How to R.E.A.C.H. Youth Today

by Manny Scott

D1056993

PAGE TURNER PUBLISHING
ATLANTA, GA

Design by Signify

Library of Congress Cataloging-in-Publication Data

Scott, Manny
    How to R.E.A.C.H. Youth Today – 2ˢᵗ ed.

ISBN-10: 1482084260
ISBN-13: 9781482084269

DEDICATION

I dedicate this book to every person who has a burden to help
the least, the last, the lost, and the left out.

INTRODUCTION

After I had finished hugging, encouraging, and taking selfies with hundreds of students, a young man, with sagging pants, tattoos on his face, and a bandana hanging out of his pocket, slowly approached me. He wasn't smiling, he wasn't looking for an autograph, and he certainly wasn't interested in taking a selfie with me. He clearly had something else in mind. With each step he took toward me, he stared straight into my eyes with a look that I had seen many times in my life. In that young man's eyes was the same hardened look that I saw among gang members and drug dealers when I was growing up on the east side of Long Beach, California. He had in his eyes the same look that I've seen in prisons among people who have been convicted of rape, violence, and murder. It is a penetrating, piercing look that searches another person's soul for any hint of weakness, phoniness, or fear.

As he approached, I noticed that he had tattoos on his neck, on his knuckles, and some scars on his hands. I greeted him, but he didn't respond verbally. He just nodded his head. Without saying a word, he handed me a big, 8 x 11-inch, yellow envelope, and just stood there.

Curious, I looked down at it, and then looked back up at him, thinking he was going to say something about it, or tell me to open it or something. Nope. Still nothing. He was silent. So I looked back down at the envelope, and flipped it over. On it was a drawing. It was a drawing of an open, upward-facing hand. In the palm of the hand was a candle, and at the top of the candle was a flickering flame. Around the wrist was a hand-cuff or or a chain.

"This is very nice! You drew this?" I asked him.

He nodded, and then said, quietly, "yep."

I told him how nice it was, and then asked him if he wanted to be an artist for living. He just shrugged his shoulders, indicating that he wasn't sure what he wanted to be.

I then made the question more broad in order to see what kind of ambitions, goals, or dreams he had. "What do you want to do with your life? What do you want to be? If money weren't an issue, what would you do for free because you loved doing it so much?"

Again, he just shrugged his shoulders, and then he looked down. I sensed that my questions hit a nerve in him. I didn't want upset him, but I wasn't in the mood to spend the rest of my afternoon trying to read his mind. "He walked up to me for a reason. Obviously, he must want to say something to me," I told myself. Still, I started to get a little impatient, and tried a more direct approach. "What does this drawing mean? Why did you draw it, and why did you give it to me?"

He looked up at me for moment, and then dropped his head. I could tell that he went somewhere mentally, and he was debating on whether he was going to tell me what he was thinking. He then looked up at me with a very intense, pained look in his eyes. He took a small step closer me. He was now about 10 inches from my face. What he said next broke my heart.

He said, "When I was little...my mom sold me to drug dealers...They raped me...and they raped me...and they hurt me." Tears started to well up in his eyes. He continued, "...and when they were done with me...they threw me in a dumpster...to die..." His voice was quietly trembling with pain. "But my brother found me," he said, pointing to his brother, who was standing in the distance against a wall, sobbing. Still pointing at his brother, "He found me...and he raised me...He's all I got...We're all we got." Tears started to well up in my eyes as I stood there in silence. Just listening.

He then grabbed the yellow envelope out of my hand. "This hand," he said, pointing at the hand in the drawing, "is my hand...And that candle is my hope." The volume of his voice began to rise with each phrase.. "It's my hope that my life can get better...my hope that I can be successful...that I can be somebody." Then he paused long enough to let all the emotion that had been bottled up inside him- emotion that he had never verbalized.

He then pointed at the hand-cuff or chain, and said, "But this chain lets me know that I ain't gonna be sh!#," as tears began to roll down his cheek. He repeated himself, "I ain't gonna be sh!#. I ain't gonna be shi!#…I wanna be something too." Before I could respond, I could tell he wasn't done. "I ain't gonna be sh!#." The pain was now pouring from his eyes, down his face, falling from his chin. His voice got softer, and you could almost see a little boy crying out for help. With almost a whimper, he said, "I wanna be something too…I wanna be somebody. But look at me. You know, I ain't gonna be sh!#."

How do you reach that young man, and others like him? How do you help someone who feels hopeless and worthless? How do you help him, and others like him, see that they do not have to be defined by their circumstances? How do you help him, and others like him, see that he does matter, and that he is somebody, and that he can overcome the obstacles in his life to achieve a life of success and significance?

I have worked in forty-seven states, in urban and rural school districts, with diverse people from very diverse socio-economic backgrounds, and I am compelled to inform you that there are young people just like that young man in every district I have visited. If you work with young people today, and have not met anyone like him yet, I bet that you will. He, and others like him, are everywhere. They are white, they are black, they are latino, and they are Asian. They are rich, they are poor; they come from two-parent homes and single-parent homes; they are drowning in despair, being suffocated by anguish, and groping for something to believe in. They are everywhere, and we must reach them.

But what does it mean to "reach" someone? I believe it means to make a connection with others in a way that results in them making positive mental, emotional, or behavioral changes. If that is true, how do we reach youth today? How do we reach the young people today who, like that young man I described above, are living beneath their potential? How do we reach the young people who are underperforming? How do we reach the young people who are living at mediocre levels, not making the most of their lives? How do we reach young men and women who are getting bad grades, who are talking back in class, who are disrespectful, and who are apathetic about the struggles and the realities of other people? How do we reach young people who are doing things in the streets that are self-sabotaging and self-defeating? How do we reach the ones getting locked up and left behind?

This book is my most up-to-date attempt to answer those questions.

For the past fifteen years, I have been on the road up to 200 days a year, speaking primarily at conventions, conferences, and schools to over 1.5 million administrators, teachers, leaders, and students. Roughly half of those audiences have consisted of middle and high school students. In the urban contexts, the students are primarily Caucasian-American, African-American, and Mexican-American. The majority of my student-audiences are living at or below the poverty line, and nearly all of them attend schools that are having a hard time reaching and teaching them.

To the delight of many school districts, my team and I have been able to reach many young people in quite meaningful ways. Not too long ago, a state superintendent of public education invited me to speak in a rural school district to about 2,000 middle and high school students. During that one hour while I was speaking at the assembly, I sensed something special happening in the room. After I finished speaking, I never have time to - and, to be quite frank, I am not even remotely interested in trying to- collect quantitative data to substantiate the effectiveness of my work through Ink International, the education consulting firm I founded.

Instead, after my presentations, I usually spend the bulk of my time talking one-on-one with students or audience members. It is during those moments when I try to encourage and counsel them, and give them advice or direction.

Interestingly enough, I returned to that school district one year later to facilitate leadership development workshops for the district's teachers and counselors. During those sessions, one of the counselors who had attended the assembly at which I spoke the year before told me that, as a result of my presentation at the assembly, forty-three students went to counselors to admit that they had been thinking about committing suicide, and admitting to needing help. How does one even begin to place a value on forty-three lives?

Through the years, I have come to see more clearly the need for organizations like mine to enter into public schools and try to do holistic work with the young people. This kind of work goes against the grain of the high-stakes testing movement going on in our country. Through Ink International, my team and I are being used to prevent suicides, and to let kids know that they are loved. We are treating them with dignity, and identifying crisis situations, and connecting them with resources that can help them flourish as human beings. As a result of our work through Ink, test scores usually do improve. However, to be honest, test scores are the least of our concerns. I'm convinced that if we address the deeper, more fundamental issues young people are facing today, then their grades will naturally improve.

Despite the effectiveness of our work with young people, some school leaders still refuse to invite us unless we give them "data" to demonstrate that Ink's work actually raises test scores. Understandably, they need something to justify them investing in us. The great tragedy, however, is that their criteria is often so narrow and truncated that it disregards the most fundamental aspects of education- the development and flourishing of the whole child. But how does one quantify hope being reborn, lives being saved, and families being restored? Many schools have no place for those kinds of measurements, and it is hurting so many kids, families, and communities.

My team and I are on a mission to help change that, and we are so grateful for all those leaders in education who are partnering with us to help their students and staff flourish. They believe in our work, and see the amazing, life-changing results that are flowing from our time in their districts.

I am seeing kids who were once thinking about dropping out of high school go to college. I have seen young people who were getting Fs and Ds turn things around academically. I have seen young people who have been molested who are now seeing themselves as survivors, living each day with more zest and purpose. I am seeing young people come to me with tears in their eyes telling me that the are no longer going to cut themselves, no longer going to disrespect teachers, or dishonor their parents. I'm seeing real changes take place, and I am so very grateful to have played a small part in those changes.

This book is my attempt to help people have that kind of impact on others, especially young people. I am no genius, and I do not have very many unique abilities that allow me to connect with, and help, people in the ways I have described. It's just that I have, through the years, learned to do a few things well. Why am I able to reach kids across the borders of race, class, gender, and sexual orientation? And, how can you reach them too? That's what I will try to answer in the remainder of this book.

In this book, I am going to do my best to share with you my philosophy and approach to reaching people. I'm going to share with you an approach that I have thought long and hard about. It is an approach I have been developing through the years, and this is the first time I have actually tried to put it down in writing. To be sure, it is a work in progress. It is not a formula. This is not a silver bullet. It is just one approach to affecting positive changes in the lives of others.

INTENDED AUDIENCE OF THIS BOOK

Although I am working on my doctorate in Intercultural Studies with a minor in Education, this book is not for the academy. I am too busy right now speaking around the country, and completing coursework, to try to write this book for scholars. While I might one day be sitting in an ivory tower, right now I am working in the trenches. This book is for those in the trenches. This work is my preliminary "data." This work, with real people, with real issues, is my research. One day I hope to take all this research and synthesize it, and present it to the academy so that teacher-training programs can improve the way they are preparing teachers-in-training. Interestingly enough, a seasoned teacher recently came up to me after my presentation, and with tear-filled eyes, said, "I learned more from you in this one hour than I learned in all my years in school. Manny, *you* are an entire teacher-training curriculum! Please keep doing what you are doing."

OUTLINE OF THIS BOOK

So, again, this book is for those in the trenches. In chapter one, then, I jump right in, giving you a glimpse into the life of someone who was considered "unreachable." I help you see life through the eyes of someone who might be very much like the young people you would like to reach. In that chapter, I ask you two of the most important questions you need to answer. Your answer to those questions will help you determine if you are even in the right line of work. Then, in chapter 2, I will introduce you to my understanding of communication 101. I have a background in Rhetoric and Communication, and want to share with you something that I believe can help improve your communication skills immediately. The diagram I share about communication will also loosely serve as my outline for the rest of the book.

In chapters three through eleven, I will spend considerable time helping you get very clear about your own frame of reference. In those chapters, I will help you to exegete your own frame of reference, and the frame of reference of your intended audience. Only once you have understood yourself as well as the person you are trying to reach, can you formulate outcomes. Only then is it appropriate to begin thinking about strategy. If you try to serve someone you don't understand, then you could very well become a benevolent oppressor. In other words, you can mean well, and still do harm. That's why I emphasize becoming a student of your students. Only once you understand them can you come up with the best, most helpful approaches to reaching them.

In chapter 12, I talk about an experience that forced me to think more critically about the concept of race. Race and ethnicity is something that needs to be talked about if you work, or plan on working, with African-American people in America today. What I learned during my research for that chapter will help you converse with others more meaningfully on such a sensitive subject.

In chapters thirteen through eighteen, I introduce you to my R.E.A.C.H. method that I have been developing over the last decade. Obviously, I call it the R.E.A.C.H. method because it spells the word REACH:

> R stands for RELATIONSHIPS.
>
> E stands for ENGAGEMENT
>
> A stands for AWARENESS
>
> C stands for CONVINCE
>
> H stands for HAND

In chapter thirteen, I talk about relationships. I am convinced we have to build healthy relationships with young people if we are going to help them create lasting changes in their lives. Those relationships can be short-term or long-term, but they must healthy and they must be real. To reach anyone, we must build relationships with them. If you are not naturally a relational person, or if you are an introvert, how can you cultivate a healthy relationship with someone that results in positive changes in their lives? In that chapter, I share ten proven principles you can begin applying immediately, and begin improving the quality of every relationship you have. When I lead my seminar on How to R.E.A.C.H. Youth Today, the discussions on relationships alone takes up a good deal of our time. I have had so many people thank me just for the information I share in that chapter.

In chapters fourteen and fifteen I talk about ENGAGEMENT. We must engage young people with activities and questions so that we can learn about who they are, and assess their needs, identify their imbalances, learn about where they are from, find out their strengths and their areas of growth. It is important for us to engage them on their level. In that chapter I share ways to capture and keep the attention of any person or audience you are trying to reach.

In chapter sixteen, I talk about AWARENESS. In that chapter I talk about how and why people change. They do not change because *we* think they have issues. They change when *they* realize they have issues. They change when *they* become painfully aware of their issues. As such, I argue that we have to help them become painfully *aware* of the imbalances in their lives. This is really important! We'll spend a good deal of time exploring this more fully.

In chapter seventeen, C stands for CONVINCE. We have to convince them that there is hope. We have to convince them that our proposed solutions can meet their needs. Our solutions can help them restore their equilibrium.

Then, in chapter eighteen, I talk about the H. The H stands for HAND. We have to extend our hand, literally or figuratively (ideally both), and ask them to make a commitment. Change begins when people make decisions. We can literally extend our hand and shake on decisions that people make; or, we can figuratively extend our hand, and be a help, an assistant, who walks with them on their journey to realizing their potential. I will share with you several ways to extend your hand to people who need to make changes in their lives.

That is what this book is about in a nutshell. As you read through this book, really slow down, and think about how these things can be applied to your own situation. Doing so will help you become a much more effective leader. I thank you in advance for your grace as you read this book. I might not say some things as effectively as they can be said, but I've done my best to put into words things that have been stirring in my heart. If something does not make sense to you, or is not very clear to you, please try to listen for my heart behind the words I employ.

One more thing. Sometimes I say this to my live audiences: as you are reading this book, if something pricks you, stop and think about it. If something causes a light-bulb to go off in your head, stop reading, pull out your journal and write.   Write in the margins. Slowly digest the things I share in this book. Doing so will be more useful to you in the long run. Don't just rush through this book to say you finished it. Mastering the things I'll lay out in this can take time. To be frank with you, I'm still working on several of these things myself. One thing I have found, though, is that the better I get at practicing the things I share in this book, the greater my impact. I believe the same will be true for you too.

In any case, I humbly request that put your heart and mind into reading this book. If you honor my request, I believe you will begin to see some real breakthroughs in your life, and in the lives of others.

-Manny Scott

PART 1: FOUNDATION

In this section, we are going to look very closely at who you are and what you bring to every encounter you have. If you are going to be effective at reaching and teaching young people, then I think you would be very wise to begin your quest by taking an inward look.

CHAPTER 1: UNREACHABLE?

I was once considered unreachable. I was born into a beautiful, but very broken, family. My father has been imprisoned my whole life. My stepfather, who was generally a good man, was an alcoholic, and he was, at one point, addicted to cocaine. There were many nights, when my stepfather got so drunk or high that he physically abused my mother. I'll never forget the night that my stepfather grabbed my mother by the back of her head, and he slammed her face through a glass window; and, as a little boy, I literally had to fight for my mother's life. There were nights when I would hear my mother screaming for help, and all I could do was call the police, and beg them to come and save my mother.

My mother, who came from a very broken family herself, tried to find stability for us- before I was 16 years old, we had already lived in 26 places–not including the cars, the beaches, the alleys, the hotels, the motels, the homeless shelters, and all the other places we stayed. I have lost count of the number of places we slept before I was 16.

There were nights that we would stop at a homeless shelter because we didn't have anywhere else to go, and I would be lying on the floor, with no pillow, no blanket, and no mattress; and I was clutching a piece of brown, stale bread, wondering why we had to sleep in places like that. Why couldn't we call family, or someone to help us?

I remember my mother taking off her jacket and, laying it over the top of me and softly saying "baby, everything's going to be okay." As much as I wanted to believe my mother, things were not okay. There were some nights when I would be so hungry that I would jump into dumpsters at Taco Bell and McDonald's, and I would tear open bags, and sift through garbage, just to find something to help me make it through the night.

I was the kid that you saw coming from a block away, who made you so nervous that you crossed the street. I was the kid with whom your parents refused to let you play. And I was the kid who took all those issues with me to school.

I used to sit in class, with holes in my pants, holes in my shoes, and holes in my self-esteem. The teacher would be assiduously covering his lesson-plan for the day, and I was sitting there, thinking about the fight I had the night before against a grown man. The teacher would be covering her lesson plan, and I'd be sitting there with sore ribs because I had recently been thrown off of a balcony. The teacher was just talking, covering her content, while I sat in class with my stomach growling, wondering when and where I was going to get my next meal.

In one of my schools, I used to sit next to the nephew of billionaire Charles Schwab (why his nephews were in my school, I'll never know). While his nephew was never mean or disrespectful to me, I could not help but notice the glaring contrast between his reality and mine. I would sit there, and wonder to myself, "why is it that everybody else seems to have new shoes, and new clothes, but my shoes and clothes are always old hand-me-downs?" "Why does everyone else have a backpack or a lunch pale, but I've never had a backpack, and I don't remember ever having a lunch pale?" "Why is it that everyone seems so happy, but I don't smile anymore?" "Why doesn't anyone want to sit with me?" And, ultimately I begin to ask "is something wrong with me?"

One day I was sitting in class after having another bad night, and the teacher asked the class a question. Like good students are supposed to do, many of my classmates confidently raised their hands to try to answer the question. But not me. I never knew the answer- sometimes I didn't even understand the question. However, for some reason, my teacher felt the need to single me out that day, and ask me to answer the question.

I felt my stomach in my throat. "I don't know," I said.

She responded, "but didn't you do your homework last night?"

"I tried, but I didn't understand it," I mumbled.

To that, she asked, in a condescending tone, "couldn't *anyone* at home help you with your homework?"

"I asked them for help, but they didn't understand it either."

She then did something that I don't think I'll ever understand. She said, "stand up." And I stood up. Then she asked, "why do your clothes look like that?"

In the spotlight of total and complete humiliation, I looked down at my clothes, then up at her, and said quietly, "I don't know."

"Don't you have a washing machine?" she continued.

"No ma'am. Well, at the-" I just stopped talking and stared at her, not knowing how to answer that question, and not really understanding *why* she was asking me that question. I stood there staring at her.

She finally ended her inquisition, and told me to have a seat.

I sat down, more self-conscious than I had ever been in my life.

Later in that same class period, she asked me to come with her into the hallway. I remember walking out of her classroom into that hallway, nervous and uncertain about what she was going to say or do- and still very embarrassed by the exchange we had just had in class. Once I got outside, she asked me those same questions, again, "why do your clothes smell like that? I can smell your clothes all the way from my desk. You guys don't have a washing machine where you live?" I said, "no ma'am." She then said, "well, I don't want you coming to my class with clothes smelling like that. The other kids are complaining to me that your clothes are stinking up the class."

Then she got closer to me, and looked me straight in the eyes, and said these words, "Young man, if you don't get your act together, and start doing your homework, you are probably going to be like your dad." With kind of a laugh or giggle, she continued, "Isn't he is prison or something?" While what she said was probably true, it did not help me in that moment. Timing and tone are everything.

I just looked up at that woman–a woman who was supposed to give me hope, a woman who was supposed to give me a glimpse of my own possibilities; a woman who was supposed to help me find my life's purpose; a woman who was supposed to love me and care for me; who was supposed to build me up, and tell me I was important– that woman scarred me deeply. I just looked up at her, and nearly in tears, I said, "yes ma'am." I went to the bathroom, and stayed in the bathroom stall for the rest of the class period.

That was merely one of many terrible experiences I've had at school. From kindergarten all the way through high school, something happened to me that made me dislike school more and more. In kindergarten, I was called in nigger. In first grade, my teacher often slapped my desk, scaring me to death, whenever I got a question wrong. She treated me as though I was stupid, and embarrassed me by constantly raising her voice and yelling at me. In second grade, my teacher often denied my requests to use the restroom even though she let the other students use the restroom. As a result, I wet my pants on more than one occasion, and had to ride the bus home smelling less than my best. In third grade, although I liked my teacher, Mrs. Elliott, I started falling further and further behind in my studies, and started noticing the huge differences between myself and my classmates. It was in third grade that I began to realize that the other kids were smarter than me, or at least they seemed smarter than me, because they always seemed to do their homework, and to always have the right answers.

And so it was in third grade that I started searching for reasons to not go to school. I faked sicknesses, I hid my shoes, I "forgot" to set my alarm, and I made up holidays, just so I would not have to go to school. In fourth grade, we moved to Long Beach California, where I was the "new kid" yet again. Being the new kid is never fun. It's scary and lonely. Being the new kid involves walking into a class, having the teacher introduce you to that class, having the class greet you, and you having to say something about yourself. In my case, I was very shy, introverted, and socially very awkward. So when I was put in those positions to speak, I was often very timid. I would often just say, "hi," sit down, and say nothing. At lunch time, I was the kid who sat alone in the cafeteria. I was the kid who got his lunch with lunch tickets, and then looked around, scanning the room, looking for a friendly or familiar face, only to find none, and ended up sitting at an empty table by himself. The loneliness, the embarrassment, the awkwardness, the self-consciousness of being the new kid always traumatized me. I got tired of not fitting in, tired of not being accepted, and tired of not being invited to join people's groups. I got tired of not being invited to birthday parties, I got tired of being on the outside. So I stopped going to school.

Instead of going home, and instead of going the school, I spent much more of my time in the streets. It was in the streets that I learned how to survive. It was in the streets, that I learned how to steal groceries from supermarkets just so I could have food to help me make it through the night. It was in the streets that I met people who were just as broken as me, just as angry as me, just as socially awkward as me, just is longing for and desirous of a place to belong like me. They were not bad people; just broken, lost people people.

I was running the streets with some of these guys, and it was then that I started smoking marijuana. It was then that I started drinking alcohol. I remember drinking a lot of peppermint schnapps, tequila, Budweiser, Old English eight balls, Bartles and James wine coolers, and a bunch of other liquor whose names I do not recall. It was in the streets that I began stealing cars and burglarizing homes and robbing people. It was in the streets, that I learned to play cat and mouse games with police officers. It was in the streets when I learned how to find secret getaways, and back streets, where I learned to identify undercover police officers and unmarked cars. It was in the streets that I learned how to survive.

I spent so much time in the streets, wasting so much time, smoking weed, getting drunk, stealing bikes, breaking into houses, doing a whole lot of dangerous and stupid things, that I practically had given up on school altogether. Really, from fourth grade to ninth grade, I missed 60 to 90 days of school, almost every year. I would be out in the streets, doing dirt, wasting time, being idle. My English grammar was so poor, and the school system was so broken, that I was placed in a classroom with immigrants who did not speak a lick of English. I sat in that class for one year trying to learn Spanish. You see, it was a class that was designed for Spanish speakers.

The first semester of my freshman year in high school, I earned a 0.6 grade point average. I earned three F's two D's and 1C. I earned a D in physical education. Nowadays, gym teachers let students where shorts that go down to their knees. But when I was in middle school, and in high school, we had to wear little tiny shorts that went up to the top of our thighs. They were like little Daisy Duke shorts; they were like little mini-shorts, the ones that had all of your business hanging out of the back! They were so short and tight, that when you put your little student-identification card in your back pocket, people could see your face through the back of your shorts. What I am trying to say is that those shorts were tiny! Also, because I had a tattoo on my left thigh–one that I received when I was eleven years old- when I drunk and high- I could not wear those little tiny shorts to gym class without getting in trouble, or being reported to the office, or, even worse, having my mother find out about my tattoo.

The second semester of my freshman year, my best friend was murdered brutally. When my best friend Alex was killed, something inside of me died with him, and I went into a very dark depression. It was in that dark place that I became very, very angry. I was suicidal. I had gotten to a place emotionally, that I really stopped caring about the feelings of other people. Emotionally, I was dead, spiritually, I was dead–everything about me was numb. And I was in such a dark place, such an angry place, that I began thinking of ways- strategizing- to make other people feel the pain with which I was living. It is indeed true that hurt people, hurt people, because I wanted to hurt people.

It was in that place of brokenness, that place of darkness, that place of death, that I just gave up–I gave up on life, I gave up on hope, I gave up on loving people, I gave up on any dreams or aspirations I thought I had. I then began saying things like, "people like me- we ain't supposed to make it!

It was in that valley of despair, that quagmire of misery, that place of utter lostness, that I gave up.

I shared all that with you to help you see life through the eyes of a young person who is lost and broken.

Let me pause right here, and ask you a question: if you saw the younger me that I have been describing on a street corner, and you wanted to reach me, what would you do? How would you try to reach me? What would you say? What could you possibly say to engage someone like the old me? If you were walking down the street, and you saw me sitting on a bench, what would you think? What would you do, if anything at all? How would you get the attention of someone who looks like he or she needs help? Think about it. Honestly, take some time, and reflect on what you would say, what you could say, or what you should say, to a young man or a young woman who was in that situation. Maybe you have already had some experiences like that. If so, what did you do? Was your approach effective? If you could go back and do it over, would you do anything differently?

TWO VERY IMPORTANT QUESTIONS

Just before I jump into the meat of this book, I have two questions I would like you to answer before we go any further. Please turn off any music that's playing, turn off any televisions that are on, and go to a quiet place. Here is the question: DO YOU HAVE A BURDEN TO HELP YOUNG PEOPLE?

History is filled with people who changed the world because they had a burden to change things. Although they were not always the smartest, richest, or strongest, they had a heavy burden in their hearts to keep fighting for their cause.

Their burden gave them the strength and inspiration they needed to keep fighting.

This leads to my second question: DO YOU BELIEVE YOU CAN HELP THE YOUTH WITH WHOM YOU WORK OVERCOME THEIR OBSTACLES? I ask this question because it is fundamental to your effectiveness as a leader. If you have all the degrees and credentials, but do not believe that your kids are greater than their circumstances, then you can't really help them. If you know all the "best practices," but do not genuinely believe that the youth with whom you work can achieve greatness, then you will be doing them a great disservice as their leader. If you no longer believe that education can equip your kids to not only realize their potential, but also become globally-minded citizens who help make this world a better place for everyone, then you cannot help them. Furthermore, if you no longer believe that the kids with whom you work can survive and thrive as productive citizens of the world, then it is unlikely that you will do the things necessary to help them achieve those things.

If you have stopped believing in your kids or in education, for whatever reason, I pray you do some soul-searching to renew your faith, or you find something else to do with your life. There is just way too much at stake for you to just be going through the motions, collecting a paycheck, and wasting your life. Our most vulnerable children and youth need leaders who are committed to showing up every day to help them flourish as human beings.

I ask again, do you have it in your heart to reach the young people of this generation? Is a burden really there, or is this just something you are doing for a paycheck? Is this some pet project, or some fad that you're getting involved with? Or, is this something that is in the very core of your heart? Is the sad situation of many young people something that bothers you? Is this something that keeps you up late at night? Is this something that sometimes causes you to cry a silent tear? Is reaching young people something that so concerns you so much that you would sacrifice your comfort, your well-being, and even your paycheck? That may seem radical to you, and it probably is, but I think that our young people today are in such a desperate situation, that they are in need of radical people who have a burden to help them, and an unwavering faith in them.

Because you picked up this book, you may very well be the kind of person who can reach these young people. I certainly hope so.

CHAPTER 2: COMMUNICATION 101

Let us begin by laying the foundation for reaching someone. A big part of reaching someone involves communication. Just because we are talking it does not mean that we are communicating. Communication involves so much more than talking. In this chapter, I want to give you a quick overview of my understanding of communication.

First, take about five or ten minutes to try to fill in the blanks that are on the diagram on the next page. It is called Communication 101, and it is tremendously helpful when thinking about the communication process, and working with others. Every word on the left side of the page should fit into a slot on the diagram itself. There are twelve words, and each word should fit into one of the twelve spots on the diagram:

1. Blame
2. Desired Action
3. Feedback
4. Frame of Reference
5. Frame of Reference
6. Frustration
7. Hearer
8. Key to Understanding
9. Message
10. Resultant Action
11. Speaker
12. Suspend Judgment

Grab a pencil, and try your best to fill in the diagram.

Communication 101

Fill in the blanks with the words below:

1. _____ Blame
2. _____ Desired Action
3. _____ Feedback
4. _____ Frame of Reference
5. _____ Frame of Reference
6. _____ Frustration
7. _____ Heater
8. _____ Key to
9. _____ Understanding
   _____ Message
10. _____ Resultant Action
11. _____ Speaker
12. Suspend Judgment

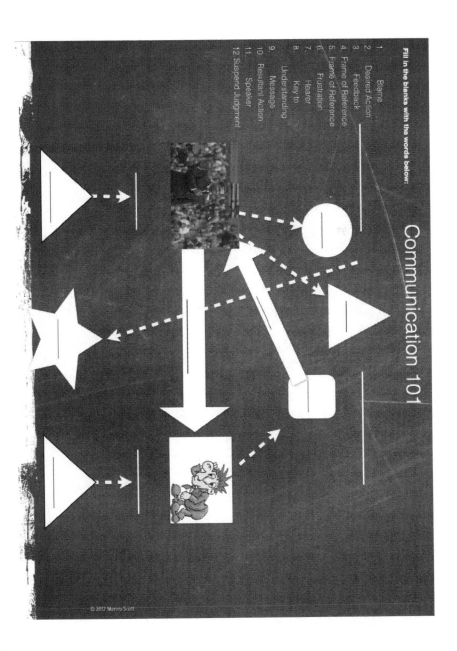

35

Now, let me show you my understanding of how the communication process works most effectively.

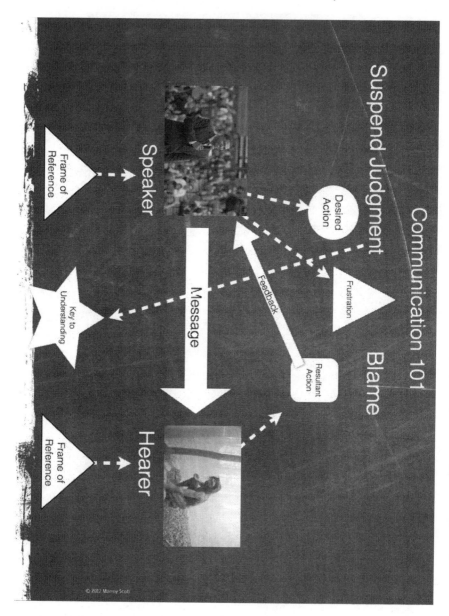

All communication starts with a Speaker. Anytime you open your mouth, you are the Speaker. As a speaker, you have a frame of reference. Your frame of reference is like a set of glasses that determines *what* you see, and *how* you see it. Your frame of reference determines *who* you see, and *how* you see them. It also determines *what* you want, and *how* you want it. Your frame of reference colors and shades the lens through which you see the world. As such, it is out of your frame of reference that you want something to happen. That is called your Desired Action (you could even call this your desired outcomes).

Out of your frame of reference, maybe you want someone to learn something, feel something, or do something. What you want them to learn, feel, or do, again, grows out of *your* frame of reference- how you see everything. However, people cannot read your mind. So you must open your mouth and deliver a Message to a Hearer.

This is usually where the communication process begins to break down. Why? Because whenever you deliver a Message as a Speaker, there are really three aspects to that message that most people miss: First, there is the message you *think* you are delivering. Second, there is the message the you are *actually* delivering. Third, there is the message that others *hear* you delivering. The message that others hear you delivering is determined by their own frame of reference. Because your Hearer probably has a completely different frame of reference from you, he or she usually learns something, feels something, or does something- Resultant Action- that is completely different from what you had in mind- your Desired Action/ Outcomes.

That Resultant Action is Feedback to you that the Hearer did not really understand your Message in the way you intended. That realization, that Feedback, often leads to the burn of Frustration; and when we are frustrated, we often respond in at least one of two ways. First, we can Blame, or we can Suspend Judgment. We can blame others for not being a good listener, or for not being smart enough, or good enough, or whatever enough. When you blame others, the problem, in your brain, is them. The problem is the Hearer. Something is wrong with *them*.

Suspending Judgment is another option we can choose whenever we feel frustration. When we are frustrated, we can work to avoid forming premature conclusions. We can withhold our conclusions until we have gathered enough information to make an informed conclusion. Rather than assuming that we have figured someone else out, or that we are certain of their motives, or that we really know what they intended, we can work to suspend our evaluation of them until we gather more information about them or the situation. We can avoid evaluating someone else's character, intentions, intelligence, or behavior prematurely. Why is that important? Because it is quite possible that the problem is not with the

Hearer, but with something or someone else. It is possible that the Message was not clear, or that the Speaker had an ill-conceived Desired Outcome.

I am convinced that it is the Suspension of Judgment that is the Key to Understanding. If we want to understand something or someone, it is imperative that we suspend judgment when we feel frustrated.

I want to show you how this works in real life. When I was in college, I met and fell in love with a beautiful woman named Alice. I was inspired to ask for her hand in marriage. So I flew to Los Angeles, secretly met with her parents, expressed my love for their daughter, and asked for, and received their blessing. Then I proposed to Alice, and she said yes. That was when all fun began. Alice was primarily responsible for planning the wedding, and I was responsible for planning the honeymoon.

I was thinking of taking her to a place with blue waters and white sand, but before I started planning, I wanted to see if there were any places that she dreamed of going for our honeymoon. I'll never forget her response. She said something like, "Well, my sister, and my cousin, and their boyfriends are all going to Italy on a ten day tour, with a big group…and the trip is going to be right around the same time as our honeymoon. So I was thinking, why don't we spend our honeymoon in Italy with them?" My heart sunk. Not because I did not enjoy the other people who were going to be on the trip, for I really believed I was marrying into one of the most wonderful families in the world. Her family wasn't the cause for my reluctance. I was just concerned that I would have to share my new bride with her family, even though it was supposed to be *our* honeymoon.

So I responded with something like, "Babe, you know I love your family. I think they are beautiful and all that. The thing is, I was thinking, though, that you and I would go some place for our honeymoon alone. Just the two of us, together. No one else. You know, the wedding vows say that we are supposed to leave and cleave, so I was thinking we could go to some exotic place, and celebrate our marriage. You know? Just us…just me and you…you and I…just us." I lost that one.

So we spent our honeymoon in Italy, with my new in-laws, and a huge group of people. On one of the first morning's of the trip, we were all eating breakfast in our hotel's dining room. My wife and I were sitting at a round table with her sister, her cousin, and a couple other people we did not know, but who were in our large travel group. The breakfast was not what I was expecting.

There were danishes that were a little different from what I prefer; the orange juice was red, which I had never seen before. There were some eggs, but they were undercooked. What was missing was some bacon or sausage- some hog! So I said to the group, "Man, I sure would like some bacon or sausage or something." One of the women at our table, who was from another country, heard me express my desire for bacon, and reached into her blouse, reached under her breasts, and pulled out a little plastic bag of meat patties! The meat patties were not in a zip-lock bag. They were in one of those little plastic sandwich bags that you flip to close. Well, her bag of meat patties had not been flipped closed. The woman reached into the little plastic bag, pulled out what kind of resembled a meat patty, reached across the table, and offered it to me. She said, in a very sweet, generous voice, "Here, please."

I could not believe what had just happened! I am not proud of what I did next, but I share it with you because I think you could benefit from my ignorance. Before I knew it, I had a disgusted look on my face, I made some kind of sound that indicated how repulsed I was, and I said, "I think I just lost my appetite." Then, to make matters worse, I pushed myself back from the table, stood up, and went back to my hotel room. On my way out of the breakfast room, I think I looked back at that woman in disbelief and disdain. Again, I am not proud of my behavior, but stick with me because I have a point to all this.

About ten years later, when I was sitting in class with friends from around the world, my eyes were opened about what had happened at that breakfast in Italy. My friend from Nigeria explained to me that some women in Nigeria have to walk long distances, and sometimes they carry their children with them. So they carry with them bags, like purses, with food, snacks and drinks to help them on their journey. My friend then gently informed me that the woman probably did not pull out the meat patties from under her "business," but rather that she had pulled them out from her purse-like bag that she wore under her clothing. Embarrassed, I began to shrink in my seat. However, it got worse.

Another friend from India said, "Manny, in parts of my country, that woman probably knew who you were, and was probably trying to bestow honor upon you." Another friend from Asia, said, "Yeah, Manny, in my country, what you did to that woman is probably one of the most disrespectful things you could have done to us." My friend from Mexico chimed in, saying, "Manny, in my country, when someone wanted something and we had it, my grandmother, and mother, always shared it with them." By the time they were done schooling me, I was so ashamed of myself. I was embarrassed. I was utterly convicted. I sat there wishing I could go back and have do-over with that woman in Italy.

Can you see how that relates to my diagram on Communication 101? As a speaker, I had a North American frame of reference. Out of that frame of reference, while I was eating breakfast in Italy, I wanted some bacon or sausage (Desired Action). I opened my mouth and expressed my desire through a Message. A woman heard me (Hearer) through her own frame of reference, and pulled out what appeared to be meat patties from under her breasts. That Resultant Action was Feedback to me, and it led immediately to Frustration and Blame. I put my car in park on Blame street. I could not believe that anyone would be so rude as to do something so socially unacceptable and uncouth. I got up with an attitude, and walked away. My mind was made up about that woman. I was her prosecutor, jury, judge, and warden.

However, had I suspended judgment that day in Italy, I could have learned something. Had I suspended judgment, I could have asked that woman a question, and perhaps made a friend. I could have learned about her country and her customs. I could have learned about her diet and her family. I could have really learned something. Furthermore, I would have probably grown as a person. However, because I was so committed to blaming her, and committed to pointing out what was wrong with that woman, I robbed myself of an opportunity to grow as a person. I delayed my own growth for ten years because my mind was closed about that woman.

You may not be in Italy, but I am pretty sure you have made the same kind of mistake in your own life. All of us, if we are not careful, can see things through our own frame of reference only, and create unnecessary walls that divide instead of bridges the unite. Whenever we encounter someone who does something that does not fit neatly into our Frame of reference, we conclude that something must be wrong with them. We need less walls and more bridges in our world. Bridges of understanding, and bridges of friendship.

Furthermore, when we encounter people and things that do not fit comfortably into our frame of reference, we tend to experience culture shock, which leads to feelings of distress, of helplessness, and of hostility toward new people and new environments.

The above communication diagram actually lays the foundation for the rest of this book. Often, when I hear people talking about helping others, and reaching others, and empowering others, and so on, I cringe, because very often the person who wants to do the helping is in need of help himself or herself. The helper is usually blind to some of his own biases that are growing out of his or her own frame of reference.

So, before we talk about reaching others, I think we need to first take a careful look at ourselves, and our own frame of reference. We all carry with us patterns of thinking, feeling, and behaving. While those patterns may not necessarily be bad, they might have unintended consequences for you when you try to reach other people. To be sure, sometimes our backgrounds are very helpful in preparing us to reach a certain group of people. Even then, though, I think it is generally better to examine our own frame of reference, because such an examination will help us become more aware of how we might be coming off to other people; and, such an analysis might help us to better understand how others might be misunderstanding us.

CHAPTER 3: FRAME OF REFERENCE

What is the ultimate purpose of life? Of education? Recently, I asked a room full of educators this same question. Their answers were fascinating. One guy started off by saying that "The ultimate purpose of life is to leave the world better than we found it." Another guy disagreed. He said, "Well, I believe the purpose of life is to experience all of the beautiful landscapes of the world. To travel." Someone else introduced his understanding of education's ultimate purpose, saying, "I believe the purpose of education is to help students realize their fullest potential." Disagreeing, someone else said, "I believe the purpose of education is to help students become world citizens so they can help humanity." We talked for another ten minutes, and their answers were as diverse as a mosaic. How do your answers compare to theirs?

Why were their, or your, answers so different? How did they all come to their conclusions? How did you come to yours? The answer is that they all had a different belief system. They all had a different understanding of the world, because of they all had different belief systems.

Our belief systems are made up of our views about the ultimate purpose of life; our deepest, core values; our short-term goals; our preferred methods to accomplish our short-term goals, and achieve our ultimate purpose; and, our understanding about how to accomplish those methods and goals. All these things together form our belief system or philosophy of life (see the diagram below). These worldviews, philosophies of life, or your belief system, are what I will loosely refer to as your **Frame of Reference**. **Going forward, I will refer to your belief system, philosophy of life, your worldview, and your frame of reference interchangeably, for it is through your belief system, or your philosophy of life, or your frame of reference that you see the world.** They color and shade the lens through which you and I see and experience the world.

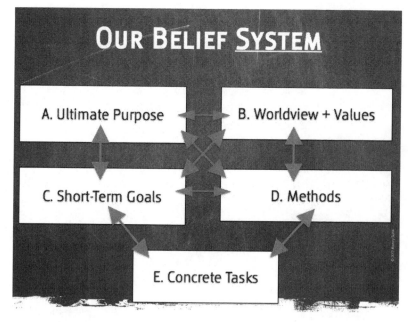

Your belief system, or your frame of reference, is so powerful in shaping your life and choices that we need to spend the next several chapters looking at it more closely.

From where does your frame of reference, belief system, or philosophy of life come? Why do you believe <u>what</u> you believe? Why do you feel the way you feel about things? Why do you do the things <u>the way</u> that you do them? I believe the answer can be found by looking at **6 things that shape** your frame of reference or belief system.

HUMAN NATURE

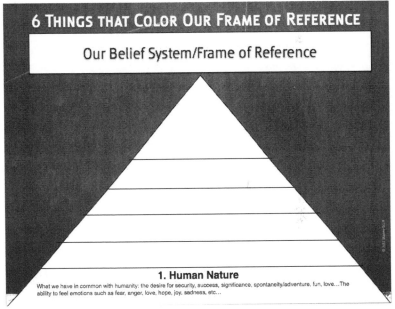

First, our frame of reference is shaped by **human nature**. Like other members of the humanity, we all have a survival instinct. We have a need to survive. We want to feel safe and secure. We want to be successful and significant. We enjoy spontaneity, novelty, and adventure. We like to laugh, have fun, and experience love. We all have the ability to feel emotions such as fear, anger, love, hope, joy, sadness, and so on.

Our frame of reference is also shaped by heredity, which I will include under human nature because they are so closely related. All of us inherited certain traits or genes from our parents and ancestors. Our eye color, our skin color, and our body types were passed down to us from someone in our family tree. We can't really change our genes. We can change how we look by getting plastic surgery or putting on makeup or contact lenses, but we cannot change the genes that were passed down to us.

CHAPTER 4: CULTURE

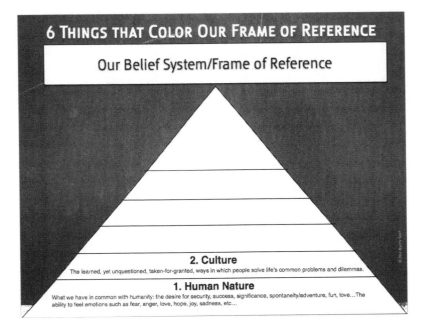

6 THINGS THAT COLOR OUR FRAME OF REFERENCE

Our Belief System/Frame of Reference

2. Culture
The learned, yet unquestioned, taken-for-granted, ways in which people solve life's common problems and dilemmas.

1. Human Nature
What we have in common with humanity: the desire for security, success, significance, spontaneity/adventure, fun, love...The ability to feel emotions such as fear, anger, love, hope, joy, sadness, etc...

"Lady, who the hell do you think you are, coming in here with all your white privilege, and your do-gooder attitude? In your brain, you probably see us all as a bunch of savages, animals, chinks, niggers, and spicks! You don't really care about us…You are just like the cops who arrested my father; you had your mind made up about us before you even got here…If you had to choose between a white person or a person of color, you know that you would pick a white person every single time."

That was essentially how several of my high-school classmates greeted our new, young, white student-teacher during her early days with us at Woodrow Wilson High School. Despite all her cheerleader alacrity, which she acquired from growing up in a gated community in Orange County, an affluent area in Southern California; despite her repertoire of "best practices" given to her by her graduate school professors; and, despite her very thorough syllabus, which had printed on it the names of some great European writers such as Chaucer, Hemingway, and Frost, my high school English teacher failed to establish a good rapport with us, her very multi-cultural, derisive class.

My high school of 3,500 students was a microcosm of Long Beach, California, one of the world's most multi-cultural cities. We had over fifty sports teams, hundreds of clubs, and a whole lot of tension. We were divided by race, class, gender, and interests. With that kind of intense diversity, how can one who works in, or feels called to work in, such a multi-cultural context serve their students more effectively?

Although many educators assume that they are effectively serving their multi-cultural classrooms, I am not so sure. Based on informal interviews I have conducted over the last decade, of local, regional, and national school leaders; and, based on the thousands of hours I have spent with diverse groups of young people, I have become increasingly convinced that many of our children might be failing in school and in life because many of their teachers do not understand them. A quick look at the dropout rates of African-American students might confirm this. In 2010, for example, 782,481 of the 2,371,154 African-American students enrolled in high schools dropped out of school. While researchers have shown that youth delinquency can be attributed to several factors (poverty, systemic and institutional racism, lack of parental involvement, etc.), my own challenging experiences with teachers in many of my public schools has prompted me to wonder how much of the problems facing youth today can be attributed to cultural misunderstandings?

If teachers lack the cultural competencies to ascertain in-depth understandings of their students, then those students who do not share their teachers' culture will be disadvantaged academically. In fact, I wonder how many students have been labeled as slow, apathetic, or have been placed in special education courses because of culture. Further still, how many of them have been suspended or expelled from school because their teachers did not take the time or develop the competencies to understand them culturally?

This is important on a practical level because if educators who work in multi-cultural schools lack a basic understanding of their students' cultural contexts, teacher effectiveness and morale will decline, teacher turnover will rise, which would exacerbate the quality of education that many kids receive America. Furthermore, there will be an increase in tension between teachers and students (and their families). Those tensions will probably lead to more suspensions and expulsions, which, in the end, will produce an increase in dropouts, teen pregnancies, an ill-equipped workforce, poverty, sickness, violence, and crime.

These concerns have prompted me to search for ways to equip educators with the cultural awareness, knowledge, and skills needed to understand, and more effectively serve, their increasingly multi-cultural students. During my quest for answers, I was fortunate enough to enroll in a doctoral-level anthropology course at Trinity International University, where Dr. Robert Priest, one of the nation's most prominent missiologists and anthropologists, led me into a goldmine of cultural anthropology, and pointed my eyes toward several gems that are sparkling there. One such gem was Glifford Geertz' (1973) semiotic approach to anthropology. In The Interpretation of Cultures, Geertz helped define what anthropology is ultimately about. While reading Geertz, I could not help but think how his approach could help improve the effectiveness of several educators who teach in multi-cultural settings.

During my presentations to audiences around the country, I often call them to become "students of their students." I encourage them "to study their students like anthropologists study culture." However, I never have time to unpack what I mean by that. So, for the next few chapters, I am going to try to explain how you can and should become like an anthropologist in your work. First, in this chapter, I will define what culture is, and then, in the next chapter, I propose that you subscribe to a symbolic approach to cultural anthropology, which I believe, can significantly help improve your effectiveness in reaching and teaching youth today.

WHAT IS CULTURE?

In <u>Teaching Cross-Culturally</u>, Judith and Sherwood Lingfelter share their knowledge about what teachers can do to become more effective at reaching and teaching people from diverse backgrounds. Their primary claim is that to be an effective teacher, one must become aware of one's own cultural values, and also understand how those values might cause conflict in other cultures. Only after one has become clear about their own biases and expectations can they begin their journey toward effectiveness as a teacher.

If culture is so important to reaching and teaching others, what exactly is culture? Culture is an agricultural word that comes from the Latin verb, *colere*, which means "to tend, guard, cultivate, or till." In most Western languages, culture commonly refers to one's cultivation or refinement through formal education. So, in most Western countries, when we say someone is "cultured," we are usually referring to someone who has an *informed* love for the music, poetry, wine, museums, and literature. This is culture in the most superficial sense of the word.

Culture, in the broader sense, refers to the taken for granted, matter of fact, _patterns of thinking, feeling, and behaving._ Let us unpack that definition a little.

Culture is patterned. There are patterns, or rituals, of thinking, feeling, and behaving that get repeated over and over again. How close should we stand to others? What should we eat? What should we not eat? Who should we be friends with? Who is not like us? When we greet each other, should we shake hands, hug, fist bump, nod our heads, say something, kiss, or bow? When we talk to one another, should we maintain eye contact, or avoid it? What about when we are talking to members of the opposite sex? How should we greet them? All these patterns give us glimpses of culture.

Furthermore, those patterns fit into a bigger historical, economic, political, and religious context. We are not a junkyard of history, but really a product of it. So, when it comes to thinking about culture, one question to ask yourself could be, "what is the nature of the order that is here?" Your answer might reveal some of the patterns of your culture.

Culture is learned. Our patterns of thinking, feeling, and behaving are not inherited genetically, but they are learned. Human beings are curiously unfinished at birth, and socialization is a part of how we learn culture.

Culture is shared. Culture is not only learned, but it is also shared with other people. Culture is learned, but it is learned by virtue of you and I being part of a community that shares that learning. It is a collective phenomenon, because it is at least shared with people who live or lived within the same social context. In that sense, culture is a collective programming of the mind which distinguishes the members of one group or category of people from another.

Another interesting thing that is important to understand about culture is that you may not always see culture, but you will feel the consequences of it if you break one of its rules. There are informal positive and negative sanctions in every culture, and if you do something that is frowned upon, then you will be punished. If you do something that is desired, then you will be rewarded. Culture, then, being a shared phenomenon, works to bring one into line. It works to make one socially acceptable among a specific group of people.

Let me try to show you how this has worked in your own life. After you were born, when your parents took you home from the hospital, they began, culturally speaking, programming you. By the way they raised you, they modeled for you how you should talk, walk, eat, greet, dress, sleep, live, love and so on. They taught you about who belonged in your group, and who did not. They taught you how people in your group should think, feel, and behave. They taught you how to properly relate to people in your family, in your neighborhood, and in your environment.

Before you even aware of it, your brain was programmed with those same patterns of thinking, feeling, and behaving. You just took those patterns for granted. Most of us never really question our patterns, because we have had them for so long. Those patterns give us glimpses of our culture.

Specifically, what kinds of patterns can you look for when attempting to understand of yourself and of those whom you serve?

Some cultural anthropologists see culture like a body with many different body parts. Just as a body has a several different parts which serve a specific function of the body, the different parts of culture serve specific **functions** for a group of people. They have identified the common problems and dilemmas that every group of people in the world faces, and how each group of people responds to those problems is what distinguishes that group as a culture. It is what sets them apart as a group. Regardless of geography or genetics, nationality, gender, ethnicity, or religion, every group of people encounters some of the following problems and/or dilemmas. Their response to these problems or dilemmas gets passed down to their children, and shapes the frame of reference of every person who grows up in that culture. In the same way, the cultural group from which you come has had to face the following dilemmas and problems, and you have been programmed to respond to these dilemmas or problems in very specific ways. Take a look at the diagram below to see my summary of the cultural problems or dilemmas that most people face:

Culture is Functional

CULTURE IS THE UNQUESTIONED, TAKEN FOR GRANTED, PATTERNS OF THINKING, FEELING, AND BEHAVING IN WHICH A GROUP OF PEOPLE SOLVES PROBLEMS AND RECONCILES DILEMMAS.

- There are are common problems/dilemmas in the world that every group of people faces, regardless of geography or genetics; of nationality, gender, ethnicity/race, age, or religion.

Low Context Cultures	High Context Cultures
Individualism: I/Me	Collectivism: We/Us
Universalism: Right	Particularism: Relationship
Low Power Distance: Equal	High Power Distance: Hierarchical
Low Tolerance for Ambiguity: Specific	High Tolerance for Ambiguity: Flexible
Neutral: calm	Affective: demonstrative
Achieved Status: Personal	Ascribed Status: Relational
Short-term Orientation: Now	Long-term Orientation: Later
Active: I can change things!	Passive: I can't change much

INDIVIDUALISM vs COLLECTIVISM

Do you believe your own interests should prevail over your family's interests; or should your family's interests prevail over your own interests? What about your school, or company for which you work? Should your own interests prevail over their interests? Or, should the school's or company's interests trump yours? What about your country? Should your own interests prevail over the interests of your country, or should the country's interests take priority over your own individual freedom? Your answer to these questions reveal the tension that exists between individualism and collectivism.

Collectivism is the belief that the interest of the group prevails over the interest of the individual; and, individualism is the belief that the interests of the individual prevail over the interests of the group. Do you do whatever you want to do regardless of how it will impact your family, classmates, company, or country? Or, do you do what is best for others, regardless of how you feel about it personally?

Both individualism or collectivism have pros and cons. The wonderful thing about individualism is that it helps the individual person reach his or her highest potential; the great tragedy of individualism is that it can lead to selfishness and self-centeredness. The beauty of collectivism is that the group grows and benefits because of the individual's sacrifice; the downside of collectivism is that the individual quells his or her own interests, and does not realize his or her full personal potential. Where do you fall on that spectrum of individualism and collectivism? I'll share some of my own journey with you.

For most of my childhood, my personal community was somewhat collectivistic, but was so dysfunctional (my father was incarcerated; my abusive, alcoholic step-father was addicted to cocaine; my extended family was not very supportive) that I slowly began subconsciously subscribing to a kind of individualism that involved me focusing solely on my own personal growth and success. Fortunately, that individualism has resulted in me doing well on a personal level (13 years of marriage, doting father of three, thriving in many areas of my life, etc.).

Having said that, I have come to see the importance of community. Like the poet John Donne said, "No man is an island, entire of itself, every man is a piece of the continent, a part of the main." Despite my own individualism, I recognize my need for community. I have in now way resolved the dilemmas, but I am trying to find a healthy balance between focusing on my own growth, as well as seeing about the needs of others in my family, my community, and my country.

I recently read an article questioning why the West is remaining silent about the way people around the world are being persecuted or suffering, and I immediately wondered how much of that silence can be attributed to individualism.

In any case, you need to become aware of where you fall on the spectrum of individualism and collectivism so that you can see how your orientation might affect your interaction with others who might come from a collectivist culture.

UNIVERSALISM vs PARTICULARISM

Imagine you are riding in the passenger seat of a car, and a loved one of yours (spouse, parent, sibling, bff) is driving the car. While riding along, your loved one accidentally runs a red light, and slams into a car in the middle of the intersection. The other car spins out of control and drive into a telephone pole, and explodes. You and your loved one are fine, even though the hood of the car you are in is a little damaged. Your loved one looks around and notices that there are no witnesses around. No one saw what happened. Without saying a word, your loved one speeds off, rushes home, and hides the car in the garage. Once inside your loved one's home, he or she turns on the television, and sees that the crash is on the news. The driver of the car that your loved one hit died at the scene, and the police are looking asking for help: "If anyone has any information about the hit-and-run, please contact us immediately."

Your loved one turns off the television in a panic, and says to you, "I know this is bad, but I just cannot turn myself in. I just can't. I will go to jail for this, and I just can't go to jail. I'm sorry." What would you do in that situation? Would you try to reason with your loved one, and try to convince him to turn himself in? If he refuses, what would you do then? Would you keep your knowledge of the accident to yourself, and not contact the police? Or, would you go straight to the police station, and let them know what your friend did? Your response to this dilemma reveals whether you are more of a universalist or a relativist/particularist.

Universalism is the belief that there are universal, objective standards in one's culture which every member of that culture ought to follow. People who subscribe to this kind of universalism generally value rules or principles over relationships. To be sure, they care about relationships; just not as much as they care about complying to the culture's universal standards. Relativists or particularists, however, value relationships over rules. They too care about rules, but just not as much as they care about preserving their relationships. This dilemma creates all kinds of conflicts in the world.

For instance, you may have seen this dilemma when it comes to marriage. When someone in your family is planning to marry someone that most people in the family do not like, does the family do anything to stop the wedding, or at least express their disapproval? Many families, despite their disapproval of the marriage, talk privately with one another about their concerns and reservations, but they almost never express their concerns with the family member whom they believe is making the "mistake." Where do you fall on that spectrum, between universalism and relativism? Would you confront the wayward family member because you felt it was your obligation to do so, or would you keep your concerns to yourself for the sake of the relationship? A universalist in that situation who believes that one should always tell the truth would perceive the family's reticence as dishonest and unloving. A relativist or particularist would care more about preserving the relationship with the relative who was about to make a mistake than they would about telling the truth. To be sure, the particularists believe in telling the truth, but just not as much as they do about protecting their relationship with their loved ones. Saying something, in the relativist's mind might upset the relative, and possibly harm the relationship.

I am not arguing for you to take any position. I am just trying to get you to get more clear about your own cultural background. This is important, because it can help you understand others who might have different cultural convictions about rules and relationships.

LOW vs HIGH POWER-DISTANCE

During my first semester at the University of California at Berkeley, on the first day of classes, a professor introduced himself to the class, and explained his expectations for the course in a manner that made me very anxious. He told us to call him by his first name, and then said, "A significant portion of your grade depends on your willingness to engage, discuss, and even disagree with me, and each other, publicly, vocally." I sat there quietly, trying to process what was saying. He continued, "I am most impressed by students who will engage in combat with me verbally. I most respect students who argue with me. If you think I am wrong, I want you to say so. Try to change my mind. Persuade me. Push back. Fight for your position." He then confessed, "I must admit that I tend to gravitate toward students who can articulate themselves well, students who are willing to disagree with me. I don't know. There is just something about those kinds of students that I just love!"

While almost all of my European-American and Asian-American classmates were used to that kind of interaction with their teachers, it became painfully clear to me that I was at a disadvantage academically. There was no way I would be able to disagree with him publicly; and, there was no way I would ever call him by his first name. Doing so would have caused me to violate some of my deepest convictions about teacher-student relationships. Most of my teachers, in high school, college, and graduate school, have had a low-power-distance orientation that made school very difficult for me, and as I look back, that may have been one of the factors that prompted me to drop out of high school.

While some of my difficulty in school may have had a little bit to do with my lack of self-confidence, I am convinced that a lot more of it had to do with power distance. What exactly is power distance?

Power distance refers to the emotional distance between subordinates and their superiors, or more specifically, to the *dependence relationship* in a country between those who are in charge and those who are under their leadership. Hofstede (2010, p. 61) defines power distance as is "the extent to which the less powerful members of institutions and organizations within a country expect and accept that power is distributed unequally." In other words, people from high-power-distance cultures subscribe to the belief that inequality exists between leaders and followers. Superiors believe that their subordinates are essentially different, and vice versa.

One's power-distance orientation begins at home. In low power-distance homes, parents teach their children to ask questions, to argue, and strive toward independence and self-sufficiency (Hofstede, 68). In many North American schools, this low power-distance orientation gets reinforced by curriculum and teachers:

> "In the small-power-distance situation, teachers are supposed to treat the students as basic equals and expect to be treated as equals by the students. Younger teachers are more equal and are therefore usually more liked than older ones. The educational process is student centered, with a premium on student initiative; students are expected to find their own intellectual paths. Students make uninvited interventions in class; they are supposed to ask questions when they do not

understand something. They argue with teachers, express disagreement and criticisms in front of the teachers, and show no particular respect to teachers outside school. When a child misbehaves, parents often side with the child against the teacher..." (Hofstede, p. 69ff).

In low power-distance homes and schools, children are encouraged to argue, express themselves, to "push back," and achieve their own intellectual independence.

Children who grow up in high power-distance homes and schools are culturally very different from ones who grow up in low power-distance ones. In high power-distance homes, children are not encouraged to become independent or self-sufficient. Instead, they are encouraged to submit to their parents for a lifetime. Their families socialize children to know their place in the hierarchy that exists in the home and in the family. Status is ascribed based on age and other facts (Hofstede, 2010, p. 67).

According to Hofstede, this hierarchy at home is reinforced in school, whereby the student sees the teacher in the same way he or she sees his or her parents (Hofstede, p. 69):

"In the large power-distance situation, the parent-child inequality is perpetuated by a teacher-student inequality that caters to the need for dependence well established in the student's mind. Teachers are treated with respect or even fear (and older teachers more so than younger ones); students may have to stand when they enter. The educational process is teacher centered; teachers outline the intellectual paths to be followed. In the classroom there is supposed to be a strict order, with the teacher initiating all communication. Students in class speak up only when invited to; teachers are never publicly contradicted or criticized and are treated with deference even outside school. When a child misbehaves, teachers involve the parents and expect them to help set the child straight..." (69)

I share this with you because unlike those who come from low-power-distance homes, students who come from high-power-distance homes experience a serious culture shock when placed in schools that reinforce low-power-distance cultures, and which have teachers with low-power-distance orientations. The people, policies, practices, and purposes in most American schools all work together to create an environment in which low-power-distance norms are often reinforced. Together, these things help to cultivate students who are independent thinkers and self-sufficient. While this is ideal, it can create significant challenges for students who come from from high power-distance environments.

But I have gotten a little ahead of myself. For now, I just want you to think about what your "power-distance" orientation is. Do you come from a high power-distance home, where you were taught that kids are meant to be "seen and not heard?" Or, did you come from a home where you were free to argue, disagree, and participate in adult conversations? In any case, your orientation definitely affects how you relate to others.

High power-distance people tend to see low power-distance people as disrespectful, whereas low power-distance people see high power-distance people as bossy and dictatorial. Let me tell you about an encounter I had with a young middle-school aged white kid in my neighborhood. Shortly after I moved into the neighborhood, I was driving home one day, and I was passing by him. I slowed down, and said, "Hello, sir. How are you?" He responded with a very informal, "wassup?" Even though I usually talk with my friends and my peers that way, I must admit that that young kids response to me took me by surprise. I couldn't believe that he was so comfortable talking to me, an adult, so informally. At first I felt disrespected, and wanted to stop the car and give the young man a lesson on how to talk to adults with respect. Then I realized that it is quite possible that either that young man had not been taught any manners, or that he was being raised in a low power-distance home where he talks like that with his parents and relatives. The more I have gotten to know that young man, I have come to see that he is actually a very friendly, helpful, smart kid who just happens to live in a home where they have a very low power-distance orientation. This realization has forced me to think twice whenever I encounter someone who comes off to me as disrespectful or too informal.

I share this with you so you can take a closer look at how your own power distance orientation might affect how you see others and interact with others.

ACHIEVED STATUS vs ASCRIBED STATUS

How do you determine someone's standing in society? How do evaluate success? Some cultures accord status based on one's personal achievements. In the United States, we as a culture tend to give status to those who have overcome significant obstacles to achieve a goal. We are impressed by people who have started from the bottom, and rose to great heights. We like hearing rags to riches stories. We are impressed by the grit, the fight, the determination that one has to have to achieve great things. We celebrate people who were once high school dropouts who return to school and graduate from college. We celebrate the person who was once homeless but who, though hard work and determination, is now rich. We are inspired by that kind of story, and we accord status because of it.

However, in some cultures, standing in society is not based on personal achievement. Rather, it is based on other factors like age, family, name, profession, education, or some other attribute. In those cultures, it does not really matter that *you* have gone to college. They are more impressed by *which* college you attended. It doesn't matter who *you* are. People are more interested in who *your father is*. People are not impressed that you work for a particular company, but they want to know your position is in that company. These examples are a bit oversimplified, but I share them with you to help you see that status in some cultures is accorded in very different ways.

If you live in the United States, chances are that you ascribe status based on personal achievement. You are more impressed by what someone has accomplished personally, regardless of who their parents are. While that is not a bad thing, it can become an issue if you are interacting with a family that does not ascribe status in that way. It is important for you to understand this reality.

LOW vs HIGH TOLERANCE FOR AMBIGUITY

Another problem or dilemma faced by every group is their ability to handle ambiguity. Scholars refer to the extent to which members of a group or culture feel threatened by ambiguous or unknown situations as "uncertainty avoidance." I refer to it as tolerance for ambiguity. Cultures that have a low tolerance for ambiguity tend to need every little detailed spelled out for them in writing, while people with a high tolerance for ambiguity do not. In the United States, we tend to have a low tolerance for ambiguity. While there are some areas where people are more laid back, when it comes to money or deals, most people need things in writing. I grew up in Long Beach, California, where most people with whom I interacted seemed to have a very high tolerance for ambiguity. However, as I have matured, I realize that when it came to getting a loan for a car or a house, the contracts are usually several pages long. I'll never forget when I bought my first home, my wife and I took over an hour to sign all of the paperwork. It was nearly unbearable.

However, in some cultures, they have a much higher tolerance for ambiguity. They don't need a 100-page contract; all they want is your word. In some cultures, a handshake is usually all the paperwork they need. If you lend someone some money, they expect you to give it back. If you don't give it back "after while," then they will probably find you to ask you for it. However, that interaction usually does not involve law enforcement, lawyers or judges.

This reminds me of The Education of Henry Adams, a book written at the turn of the 20th century by Henry Adams, the grandson of US President John Quincy Adams. Written during a time in which many changes were taking place in the world, Adams came to the conclusion that his education had failed to prepare him for the social, technological, political, and other changes that were taking place in the world around him. Even though I read the book once during my college days in the late 1990s, one sentence from the book has remained with me through the years: "Chaos is the law of nature; order is the dream of man." One could argue that the high-uncertainty-avoidance culture in which Adams was raised had failed to help him make sense of all of the ambiguity in the world.

I've also realize that some of my frustrations in my own work have grown out of my own desire to have everything under control. However, there have been times when I have had to reconsider my proclivity for structure and specificity. For example, once, when I was putting together an agenda with a colleague who came from a culture that had very high tolerance for ambiguity, I asked him what he wanted to do during a sixty-minute slot of time. With a straight face, he said something like, "I think I'll just go with the flow." I laughed, thinking he was joking. He wasn't. He said, "I'm just gonna go with the flow." I responded, "I can't put that on the agenda. I need something more concrete." He laughed, and said, "No, just put down: 'go with the flow'" Against my low tolerance for ambiguity orientation, I ended up putting those words on the agenda. Then, during the meeting, when we got to the "go with flow" item on the agenda, he flowed very naturally and powerfully. While watching him, I was reminded that there are some things that my own preference for specificity came from my cultural background.

What is your own orientation when it comes to ambiguity? When you plan for a trip, do you need all the details planned out before you leave home, or do you go with the flow? Your cultural background probably has something to do with that.

NEUTRAL vs AFFECTIVE

Another aspect of culture involves emotions. When you talk on the phone, do your hands rest at your sides, or do they move around during your conversation? Do you talk with your hands? When you are listening to music, do you tend to sit still, and just enjoy the music cognitively? Or, when a song comes on, do you start to move with the music? Do you feel an inclination to dance?

Years ago, my wife and I attended a concert at Westminster Abbey in London, England. The boy choir sang some beautiful songs while standing completely still. They did not clap, they did not rock, they did not dance. They just stood there and sang. The audience just sat there too. After each song, the audience politely applauded, and then the room fell silent again. It was beautiful, but it was very different for me and my wife. It was different for us, because, culturally, we come from a more emotionally affective cultures than our friends in London. My wife and I were used to choirs clapping, and swaying, and dancing, and moving. We were used to the audience standing on their feet singing along with the choir, and participating in the experience. Neither that choir's performance nor our expectations were wrong, they were just different.

This distinction is important because people who come from emotionally neutral cultures tend to see people who are emotionally affective as thoughtless. They sometimes look down upon people who express themselves with emotion. They see emotion as a distraction. Conversely, people who come from emotionally affective cultures tend to see people from neutral cultures as heartless and boring. People from affective cultures have hard time listening to speakers or singers or performers who are not demonstrative and passionate and emotional in their presentations. If they are not raising their voices, or personally and obviously involved in what they are doing, then, from the affective person, that performer "must not believe" what he or she is saying or performing.

If you attend a black Baptist or Pentecostal church on any given Sunday, you will usually experience a choir singing with its whole being. They are sometimes sweating, swaying, singing, and rocking with all that they are. Some people who come from neutral cultures sometimes see that kind of worship as too emotional and distracting.

If you attend a white Presbyterian church on any given Sunday, you might find the choir sitting in the back of the congregation. My professor told me that his choir sits in the balcony, behind the congregation. When I asked him why, he explained that in their context, the audience would rather listen to the ideas being expressed through song, and listen to the notes being sung or played. To see the choir would only be a distraction. People who come from emotionally affective cultures would probably see that arrangement as unusual and uncomfortable.

I share this with you so that you can determine if you come from a neutral or affective culture. I may return to this later, but I should say it now. If you are working with emotionally affective people, then you need to work at being more demonstrative in your interactions with them, because if they can't feel you, it will be hard for them to hear you. Even if you are an introvert, you can still be personally involved in what you are saying or singing. This is just a cultural reality.

SHORT-TERM vs LONG-TERM ORIENTATION

There is another problem or dilemmas that cultures face that refers to time. Cultures with a long-term orientation foster virtues oriented toward future rewards, while cultures with a short-term orientation foster virtues related to the past and present. Some scholars also make a distinction between sequentially-oriented people and synchronically-oriented people. The former have a proclivity to only do one activity at a time, while the latter have the ability to several things at once, like a juggler.

What is your orientation towards time? Are you short-term or long-term orientated? Do you have a tendency to rush things, and need things done right away? Or, do you have long-term goals that you know will require a lot of hard work, patience, sacrifice, and dedication?

The United States is generally very short-term oriented, and has a lot of citizens who have a hard time delaying their gratification. If we want something, we want it now. We have fast-food restaurants, with drive-thru windows, because we are always in a hurry. We don't like waiting in lines, we don't like waiting for results. We want everything now.

In some cultures, however, people have a longer view of things. They have very long term goals, and realize that it is going to take a lot of time, maybe even decades, or centuries, to achieve those goals. I am sitting in Paris, France right now as I write this chapter, and cannot help but marvel at the fact that Notre Dame took almost 200 years to build. I will be headed to Milan, Italy in a few days to see its Duomo. That magnificent cathedral took almost 600 years to build! Even the way they eat dinner in French and Italy is much slower. Generally, the waiters are in no rush to bring out your meals. In the United States, waiters often bring out your entree while you are still eating your appetizer. At a restaurant here in Europe, my wife and I were finished with our appetizer, and were just sitting at our table waiting for our entrees to be served. The waiter kindly approached us and asked us if we were ready for our meals. She did not want to rush us. Instead, she was giving us time to enjoy the appetizer and our conversation. During our travels to Europe, we have come to see that many countries here see meals as opportunities for people to converse and connect. If you have a short-term time orientation, you might have a hard time adjusting to those who have a long-term orientation to the world.

ACTIVE vs PASSIVE

How does the culture from which you come see the world in which we live? Is there a sense that the world is so complicated, and multifaceted, and intertwined that it is nearly impossible to change anything? Or, were you raised with a sense that you have the power to change the world? Your response to this reveals your orientation toward nature. Some have an active orientation and others have a passive one. Those with passive orientations see themselves as very small elements in the world, and that their own actions can do very little to change things. Those with an active orientation, however, believe that although they may be small, they have power within to affect the environment, and make changes in the world.

What is your orientation toward the world in which you live? Do you think things are going to stay the same no matter what you do, or do you really believe that you can change some things? In the United States, we tend to have an active orientation when it comes to change. There are several cultures within the United States, however, that have a more passive orientation to the world. Some people have been poor for so long, and have endured so much, and have been beaten down by so many, that they do not really believe that they can change anything.

I share this with you because you need not assume that everyone around you believes that they have the power to make a difference in this world. They don't believe that they can change anything, not even their own situations. Before you can help them, you need to understand that it is not a given that people believe they can change their environment or the world around them.

HIGH-CONTEXT vs LOW-CONTEXT

I need to say one other thing about understanding how culture shapes your frame of reference. In <u>Beyond Culture</u>, Edward T. Hall introduces the terms "high-context culture" and its contrast, "low-context culture." These concepts help us place all of the above variables like power-distance and individualism into two broad categories. High-context culture refers to a culture's tendency to use high-context messages in routine communication. In a higher-context culture, many things are left unsaid, letting the culture itself do the explaining. In such settings, people do a lot more communicating with body language, and facial expressions, and sometimes tones of voice and sounds than they do with actual words. Since a few words can communicate a complex message very effectively to an in-group (but less effectively to outsiders), words and word choice become very important in a high-context environment.

In a low-context culture, the communicator needs to be much more explicit, and the value of a single word is less important. In low-context contexts, then, less is said through cultural symbols, sounds, gestures, and body language, and more is said through the use of actual words.

This choice between speaking styles indicates whether a culture will cater to in-groups, which is a group that has similar experiences and expectations. In the cockfighting story I will share later in the book, you will see how the Malinese people were very high-context. For now, though, I just wanted to give you some terms to help you describe some things that you have probably encountered, but perhaps didn't know how to describe.

Culture is often functional. It is a group's attempt to solve problems and reconcile dilemmas in its unique context. That is one way to look at culture. This is helpful because whenever you are interacting with someone from a different culture, and you encounter something that does not make sense to you, it would not hurt to run their ideas, feelings, or behaviors through the above grid of variables to see if things become more intelligible to you. I am not saying you need to agree with what you are seeing. Rather, I am proposing that you first seek to understand before you analyze or evaluate, and the above concepts help us do that more effectively.

CHAPTER 5: THICK DESCRIPTION

The previous chapter described culture as functional. This chapter shows that culture is also symbolic. In The Interpretation of Cultures, Glifford Geertz, an American anthropologist, comes to our aid when thinking about how to more effectively reach youth today. In his essay, "Thick Description: Toward an Interpretive Theory of Culture," Geertz asserts that the concept of culture is symbolic, saying,

> "The concept of culture I espouse…is essentially a semiotic one. Believing, with Max Weber, that *man is an animal suspended in webs of significance he himself has spun, I take culture to be those webs, and the analysis of it to be therefore not an experimental science in search of law but an interpretive one in search of meaning.* It is explication I am after, construing social expressions on their surface enigmatical."

Culture, in his view, is a system of symbols. A **symbol**, is an object, sound, action, or idea to which people arbitrarily assign meaning, and there is no necessary relationship between the symbol and its meaning.

The meaning of a symbol *is only recognized by those who share the same culture*. That is why Geertz claims that symbols on their surface are "enigmatical." He argues that all human thinking, feeling, and acting is symbolic:

"Once human behavior is seen as…symbolic action-action which, like phonation in speech, pigment in painting, line in writing, or sonance in music, signifies….The thing to ask is what their import is: what it is…that, in their occurrence and through their agency, is getting said." (p. 10)

By seeing people, and their words, their gestures, articles, and clothes- every aspect of their lives- as symbols that have a deeper meaning, people's lives become like ink on a page, or words in a manuscript, or like an "acted document," which ought to be carefully read, if they are to be understood. He disagrees with those who say that culture is a *power* that causes people to behave in certain ways, and instead argues that culture is better seen as a *context* that helps us understand peoples' patterns of thinking, feeling, and behaving.

Geertz then extends his metaphor even further. He claims that since people are like manuscripts that should be carefully read, they are also like books which should be "thickly" described. Culture, Geertz says, "is a context, something within which [symbolic discourse] can be intelligibly- that is, thickly- described." Although I do not fully agree with Geertz that culture is not a power that creates or causes (for culture, through social hierarchies, hegemonic power, and ethnic stratification, does, and has changed language, and inspired resistance), I fully endorse his final conclusion that culture is a context through which all social action can be grasped.

If culture is symbolic, or an "acted document" that must be read, or a "context" that makes social action intelligible, then it is imperative for the anthropologist (or in our case, educators or youth workers) to find ways to read those texts (or construct a reading of them). That is the primary task of anthropology, and educators *using the tools of* anthropologists. As such, ethnography the subject to which we now turn.

"THICK DESCRIPTION"

One of the key terms in Geertz's symbolic framework is "Thick Description." According to Geertz, the primary task of anthropologists is to do ethnography, which is "thick description." He says,

> "Ethnography is thick description. What the ethnographer is doing is in fact faced with...is a multiplicity of complex conceptual structures, many of them superimposed upon or knotted into one another, which are at once strange, irregular, and inexplicit, and which he must contrive somehow first to grasp and then to render.....Doing ethnography is like trying to read (in the sense of 'construct a reading of') a manuscript- foreign, faded, full of ellipses, incoherencies, suspicious emendations, and tendentious commentaries, but written not in conventionalized graphs of sound but in transient examples of shaped behavior." (p. 10)

Anthropologists do ethnography, and ethnography is "thick description." In other words, Geertz believes that anthropology's primary task is to explain cultures through thick description, which *should entail not only describing a behavior, but also its context, in such a way that the behavior becomes meaningful, or intelligible, to an outsider.* Why is that important?

The significance of thick description is that it supplies a means by which leaders who work with youth can "expose a culture's normalcy without reducing its particularity (p. 14). The knowledge we gain from thick description allows people access to "another country heard from" (p. 23). One of the primary purposes of creating thick descriptions is *to help people see how others see the world.*

"Thick Description" specifies many details, conceptual structures and meanings in order to give someone who is not a part of that culture a framework through which to make sense of what is going on. *It should contain not only facts but also commentary, interpretation, and interpretations of those comments and interpretations.* The ethnographer's, or educator's task, is to extract meaning-structures that make up a culture because a factual account alone is insufficient. The meaning-structures within a cultural context are layered in a complex way - one meaning-structure is so intricately intertwined with another meaning-structure that each fact or "symbol" might be subjected to intercrossing interpretations.

It is these meaning-structures that anthropologists should study, for without a knowledgable understanding of those meaning-structures, the ethnographer is left with nothing more than a "thin description," which is a factual explanation of some behavior without an interpretation of that behavior to help people understand its deeper meaning. Put simply, **"thick description** *is the rendering (explaining to others through writing) what the symbols of a culture mean from the point of view of the people who are a part of that culture.*

One of the implications of producing a "thick description" of a culture is that an anthropologist must first try to *grasp* (see/understand) a culture's structures of meaning before he or she tries to *render* it. Furthermore, in order to grasp, one of the elementary prerequisites of anthropology is to do one's best to *interpret things from the actor's point-of-view (as opposed to the participant-observers')*. However, in order to grasp an insider's understanding of a symbol or culture, an anthropologist ought to strive to converse- speak *to* or *with-* the people of a culture, before he or she tries to speak *for* them. Geertz agrees, saying,

> "We are not, or at least I am not, seeking either to become natives (a compromised word in any case) or to mimic [a groups culture]. Only romantics or spies would seem to find point in that. We are seeking, in the widened sense of the term in which it encompasses very much more than talk, *to converse with them,* a matter a great deal more difficult, and not only with strangers, than is commonly recognized." (p. 34)

In order to learn about the structures of meaning within a culture, the ethnographer must learn to speak the host culture's language. It is doubtful whether one can be bicultural without also being bilingual. Words are vehicles of culture transfer. Without knowing the language, one will miss a lot of the subtleties of a culture and be forced to remain an obvious outsider.

To grasp a cultural context, one must not only learn to speak to the people that culture, ethnographers should aim to study *in* places, not *about* them. Geertz confirms this, asserting, "The locus of [an ethnographer's] study is not the object of study. Anthropologists don't study villages (tribes, towns, neighborhoods...); they study *in* villages" (p. 22). This has tremendous import for educators that I will discuss momentarily.

By doing these things, and thinking about them in the above manner, an anthropologist (and educator) can increase his or her chances of obtaining a "thick description" understanding of a culture. Despite the fact that an ethnographer's knowledge will grow in "spurts" (p. 25), and he will never get "to the bottom of things" because cultural analysis is intrinsically incomplete (p. 29), anthropologists must still work toward gaining a first-person, actor-oriented perspective of symbolic action. Geertz reassures, that while one's interpretations may not be completely accurate, "it is not necessary to know everything in order to understand something." (P. 20) When constructing a reading of a person or culture, the ethnographer is doing his or her best to understand *something* of the webs of significance that a group of individuals have themselves constructed.

In his essay entitled, "Deep Play: Notes on the Balinese cockfight," Geertz provides an example of what thick description looks like. Read this carefully, because it gives you a sense of how you too can work in your own context to gain a thick-description understanding of your youth. Geertz describes the ritual of cockfighting that he and his wife observed as anthropologists in Bali in 1958. Upon their arrival, the people of Bali ignored them. Despite their best efforts to establish some kind of rapport, which he refers to as the "mysterious necessity of anthropological field work" (p. 416), the people of Bali ignored them. In the eyes of the Balinese, they had not yet achieved the status of "existence." Though the Balinese were aware of what Geertz and his wife were up to, they chose not to acknowledge, or even interact meaningfully, with the outsiders (p. 413). These informal negative sanctions indicated a form of rejection, or perhaps neutrality, toward outsiders.

Ten days into their visit, they attended a cockfight. Cockfighting, with the exception of a few events, was illegal in Bali at the time. His first observation of the cockfight was raided by the police. Instead of identifying themselves to the police as guests, and distancing themselves from the people participating in the cockfight, Gertz and his wife ran away from the police like the Balinese villagers. The Balinese locals interpreted the running of Geertz and his wife as a demonstration of solidarity, as an affirmation of the Balinese way of life. That gesture (running) transformed Geertz and his wife from invisible, "gusts-of-wind" (p. 413) into the accepted "co-villagers" (p. 416). "[Running from the police] led to a sudden and unusually complete acceptance into a society extremely difficult for outsiders to penetrate" (p. 416). That acceptance was marked by the villagers teasing Geertz and his wife (p. 416).

With this newfound acceptance into society, Geertz began an exploration of the cockfights in detail. In doing so, he discovered that cockfighting was such an intense portrait of Bali life that Balinese compared heaven to the mood of a man whose cock has just won, and hell as the metaphysical and social suicide of the loser (p. 421). Not all cockfighting was considered this important, however. Rather, Geertz suggested that there were times—what he called "deep play"—when both parties in the cockfight entered a relationship likely to bring net pain (p. 433). Geertz found it interesting that, although some might argue this deep play is unethical, Bali men passionately and repeatedly partook in these activities. As such, cockfighting—and the betters who participated—formed a "socio-moral hierarchy" (p. 435). The cockfight is a symbolic revelation of what Balinese "are really like." As much of America surfaces in a ball park, on a golf links, at a race track, or around a poker table, much of Bali surfaces in a cock ring. *For it is only apparently cocks that are fighting there. Actually, it is men."* (p. 417).

Through a very microscopic analysis of Balinese webs of significance, Geertz asserts that the cockfight is a ritual through which Balinese men and their social groups channel their rivalries, and compete for prestige and status. He argues that although gambling occupies a central role in the Balinese cockfight, there is a lot more at stake in the cockfight than economic reward. When it comes to the cockfight, prestige and status are much more important than money. To illustrate his point, Geertz describes the distinction between "deep fights," which involve high wagers, and "shallow fights," which involve low wagers. A "deep fight" is a fight in which the stakes of status and prestige are so high that people lose their rationality. The cockfight is a fight for status, and the wagers being placed merely function to symbolize that risk is involved. Although participants in the "deep fights" are usually influential members of a society, the cockfights are not between individuals, but rather between social groups. The cockfight is a simulation of social structure as well. People do not make wagers against a cock that represents their own groups. The cockfights always involve a battle between people from opposing social groups. *In that way, the cockfight is the most pronounced expression of a rivalry between two social groups, and it is an important, symbolic way through which the Balinese people ventilate such rivalries.*

Whether a cockfight ends in victory or defeat, the status that a Balinese gains or loses as a result of the fight is only temporary. One's overall status in the group is not permanently damaged. Like the status an American football fan who may get teased because his team has lost a big game, Balinese men essentially maintain their overall status in their communities. With every cockfight, there is an opportunity to regain, or reassert, one's supremacy. So just as a North American football game is just a football game, a cockfight, in the grand scheme of things, is just a cockfight.

The "deep play" of the Balinese cockfight, says Geertz, is like a piece of art which illustrates an essential insight into our very existence. The art is a symbolic manifestation of something we perceive to be very real in our social lives. It is a channel through which we ventilate our emotions and understandings of ourselves and the world around us. Thought about in that way, then, the cockfight symbolizes, and participates in shaping, the social and cultural structures of the Balinese people

Geertz concludes that rituals such as the Balinese cockfight are like a text which can be read and understood, even if the text consists of a chicken hacking another mindlessly to bits (p. 449). He says, "[t]he culture of people is really an ensemble of texts, texts which are themselves ensembles which the anthropologist strains to read over the shoulders of those to whom they properly belong (p. 452), and recommends that on whatever level anthropologists decide to read these texts, societies and lives contain interpretations to which one must learn how to get access.

IMPLICATIONS FOR REACHING YOUTH TODAY

Geertz' manner of analyzing a culture is extremely useful because it sheds light on how those who work with youth might consider entering, reading, and describing the culture of those youth. I have identified at least four implications that, if embraced by leaders who work in multi-cultural settings like my high school, could aid them in their quest to engage, reach, and teach more students.

1. See Students as Actors

One implication of Geertz approach is that educators would do well to see their students as actors of (cultural) scripts. Over the last fifteen years, I have asked school administrators about the biggest challenges they face in their schools, and I have lost count of how many times someone has said their teachers were their problem, namely, *how* their teachers held unhealthy views of their students. I think Geertz' metaphor, of seeing students as actors of a script could serve as a healthy corrective for teachers who have a tendency to inappropriately label their kids. For example, if teachers began to see that every one of their students (and everyone else with whom they come into contact) is acting out a script of learned, shared, integrated, patterns of thinking, feeling, and behaving, they would probably approach their students, and their jobs, a little differently.

Perhaps they would be more hesitant to dismiss, ignore, or punish some students. Understanding that what teachers were seeing was merely a reflection of an unseen web of significance, teachers could begin to see that perhaps their first job as a teacher is to become a student of their students. Teachers would see their need to learn more about the contexts in which their students were raised. If teachers would humble themselves in that manner, I believe they would begin learning things about, from, and with their students.

2. Search Symbols for Meaning

A second implication flows from the first, namely, those who work with youth should constantly be studying symbols and their meanings. Most anthropologists I have read agree that cultures constantly adapt to the changing world around them. As a result, the meanings that cultures give to symbols is also dynamic. To learn about the interpretations of these symbols, teachers would do well to frequently ask, "what does that mean?", "What is the nature of the order that is here?" What are some patterns?"

Teachers and leaders should be asking their students questions about the meaning of their symbols, heroes, and rituals. What music do they listen to, and why? Who do they admire, and why? What are they wearing, and why? Why are some students wearing Cortez Nikes (attire for the East Side Longos, a Latino Gang in Southern California)? What might that mean? Why are some students wearing grey (attire of the Tiny Raskal Gang, a Cambodian gang), and what does that mean? Why are some students sagging their pants, and what does that mean? Why are so many African-American young men wearing extra-large white T-shirts? What does that mean? What tattoos do they have on their bodies? What do those tattoos mean? What might they be trying to communicate through such art? Of all the tattoos they could have gotten, why did they choose that one? Geertz has helped me see that these kinds of questions can help teachers begin to understand the students who show up in their classrooms every day.

Indeed, such questions can help teachers understand how their students see themselves, others, and the world around them. The more questions a teacher asks, and the more answers they receive, the greater their chances of learning and understanding their students.

I think this manner of asking questions is also helpful because, long before I had heard about semiotics or Geertz, I learned that some symbols had potentially deadly consequences. For example, in my neighborhood, the color red was tied to the Bloods, a street gang that began in Los Angeles and is now all over the country. The color blue was worn by their rivals, the Crips. If one wore a red hat, or red jersey, and walked, or drove a red car, in an area where some Crips resided, then a Crip in that neighborhood would have probably interpreted those things as a threat, or as an intentional encroachment upon their territory. Either of those things would have been seen as the ultimate sign, or symbol, of disrespect. Even though one's love for red might have had nothing to do with gang membership, by wearing red, that person could have unknowingly put himself at risk being of confronted, assaulted, or even killed.

For someone who did not grow up in neighborhoods like mine, they might deem that unfathomable. However, Geertz' semiotic approach gives educators, and anyone who works with youth, a way to make such behaviors more clear and intelligible. That kind of understanding is something that is greatly needed in public schools today.

3. Acknowledge the Proximal Nature of Interpretations

This leads to a third, related, implication. Educators need to acknowledge that their interpretations of their students *are,* in fact, interpretations. In order for teachers to effectively teach in multicultural contexts, they need to understand how their own assumptions, interpretations, and evaluations of others have been shaped by their own cultural backgrounds. I believe that this kind of self-awareness could also help teachers identify any bias or prejudice he or she might have about students. Duane Elmer, a former professor at Trinity

International University once described this kind of ethnocentricity much more eloquently during one of his lectures, affirming,

"There is a fine line we unconsciously cross that causes the majority of [intercultural] problems. When we think we are *normal*, we make the rather fatal slip into believing that we are also *the norm* by which everything and everyone else can be judged. We do this without thinking. But every time we make a negative attribution we risk saying rather loudly to those around us, 'That's not like me, therefore it is inferior, wrong and unacceptable.'"

Leaders need to work to make sure their interpretations are as close to the interpretations of their students as possible so they can help reduce the potential for cultural misunderstanding, or worse, cultural chaos. This leads to the final implication I would like to discuss.

4. Strive to Speak *To* Before Speaking *For*, or *About* Youth.

My high school English teacher once said that she was trained to teach by professors who had not seen a kid in *over one-hundred years*. She had professors teaching her about students even though they themselves had not recently spent any time with students. As a result, my teacher had to learn about teaching in our multi-cultural school the hard way- trial by fire. Realizing that none of the methods she had been taught to use on us were working, she humbled herself and spent time trying to get to know us. Although she began as an outsider, her humility, and her loving manner demonstrated to us that she valued us, and respected our cultures. As a result, we let her in, and accepted her.

She visited our homes, and got to know our families. She asked us to give her tours of our neighborhoods, and even asked us to introduce her to some of the neighborhood drug dealers! She listened to us as we discussed our heroes, our music, and our cultures. Because of her commitment to enter our world, the magic of learning began to take place in our classroom. I believe that if educators adopted that kind of approach- spending time *with* their students, *in* their contexts, and talking *to* them-, teachers would become much better informed, and qualified, to talk *for* and *about* their students with others. This is not insignificant.

When teachers earn the trust of their students in that way, their students will begin to share relevant, sometimes insider, knowledge with them. Teachers who spend quality time *with* their students, *in* their contexts, have a much greater chance of learning about things that could have transformational significance.

As a result of reading this chapter, it is my hope that all teachers would adopt an anthropological approach to culture, really becoming students of their students, and effectively studying them like anthropologists study culture. By doing so, I believe you will begin to identify patterns of thinking, feeling, and behaving that give you clues to their unique webs of significance.

CHAPTER 6: FIVE CIRCLES

In the last several chapters we talked about your frame of reference, and especially about how your culture shades how you see the world. But how exactly do you identify whether someone is an individualist or collectivist? How can you tell whether they have a low tolerance for ambiguity, or whether they are active or passive? How can you get at someone's belief system or their core values? I have found the below diagram with concentric circles to be helpful.

In the diagram, there are five concentric circles. The outer three layers give us a glimpse into the inner two layers. Because you cannot see someone's beliefs or values by just looking at them, all you can do is look at their symbols, heroes, and rituals.

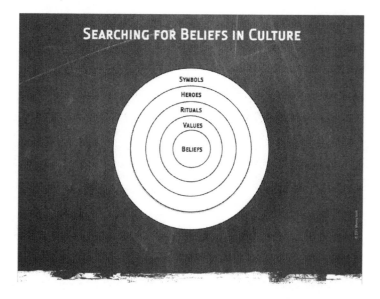

SYMBOLS

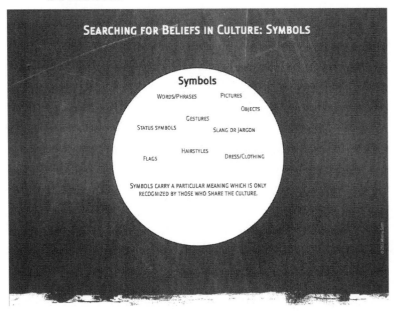

Let us start with symbols. Symbols are words, sounds, gestures, or objects that mean something that is only recognized by those who share the culture. The words in a language, including slang or jargon would fit into this group. Jewelry like wedding rings and necklaces are symbols. Tattoos are also symbols. Clothing and hairstyles also fit here. What people drink, and the colors they wear, or the bandanas they have on, or the flags they fly are all symbols. The kind of cars that they drive, or the kind of homes the live in, are symbols of something much deeper.

In some neighborhoods, the color red is tied to the bloods, and the color blue is tied to their rivals, the crips. If you go into certain neighborhoods wearing the wrong colors, you could very well become a target. If you wear a red hat, or red jersey, or are driving a red car in an area where crips reside, then they could interpret your presence as a threat, and as a sign of disrespect. They could see you as intentionally encroaching upon their territory. Even though you might just like red, and are not affiliated with any gangs, that does not necessarily change how you will be seen in certain neighborhoods.

Symbols within cultures are fluid. New symbols are easily created and established ones fade away. Another fascinating thing about symbols is that symbols from one cultural group are often copied by others. Because they are so easy to adapt and copy, symbols are the most superficial way of identifying someone's deeper values and beliefs. That is why symbols are on the outer later of the diagram.

The main thing you want to ask yourself when you see symbols is what might this symbol mean to this person? Let us use a tattoo as an example. When you see someone with a tattoo, chances are they were trying to express something about their deeper values and beliefs. Even if you don't understand what the tattoo means, ask yourself, "what might this person be trying to communicate to the world about his or her deepest values and beliefs?"

HEROES

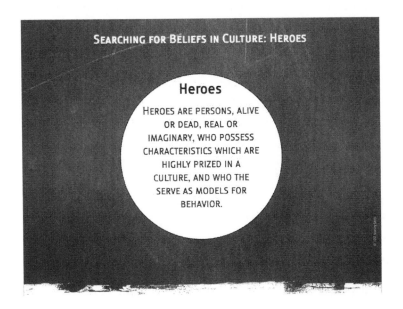

Heroes are the next layer of culture that we can observe in order to determine someone's deeper values and beliefs. Heroes are people, living or deceased, actual or fictitious, who have attributes and characteristics that are highly valued in a culture, and who serve as role models for behavior. Even cartoon characters and people from fantasy books and movies can be heroes. Batman, or Harry Potter, or Heath Ledger, or Tupac Shakur, or Beyonce, or Slipknot, or Vicente Fernandez, or Pele the soccer player might all be heroes to someone. The question you need to ask yourself is what is it about this "hero" that this person values or venerates? Why is this person a hero?

Not too long ago, a teacher who grew up in the suburbs of a nice homogenous town, and who is a new teacher in a diverse, poor, inner city school, told me that one of her students told her that his mother, who was in jail, is his hero. Then, perplexed, she asked me, "Why would anyone consider his imprisoned mother a hero?" While I understood her question, I also understood how that student saw his mother as a hero. That mother, despite her being locked up, could still very well be that boy's hero for any number of reasons: maybe she was defending herself against a violent boyfriend, but could not prove that it was self-defense; maybe his mother had been through so much in life, but instead of giving up, she has fought to keep her family together. Maybe she is a hero because she is the strongest person he has ever met. Maybe she is his hero because she has overcome some of life's most difficult circumstances, and is still alive. Without digging deeper, it is easy to question why anyone would consider a prisoner a hero. However, if you go deeper, you might very well find very little that is worthy of veneration; or, who knows, you might find something that is quite honorable and inspiring.

Growing up, I loved Tupac Shakur because he gave a voice to my anger and frustration as a young man growing up in the inner city. I also looked up to Snoop Doggy Dogg because he had a swagger that I wanted. He was just so smooth. I used to have posters of Jerry Rice on my wall because I wanted to be a great football player. I used to watch Rambo over and over again, because I loved how he was a loner who could survive even in the most life-threatening circumstances. My heroes expressed my deepest struggles or aspirations.

Who are some of your heroes, and why? What is it about them that inspire you? Your heroes are a clue to some of your deepest values and beliefs.

Who are the heroes of your kids? Who do they look up to? Who do they venerate? Who do they emulate? Why?

RITUALS

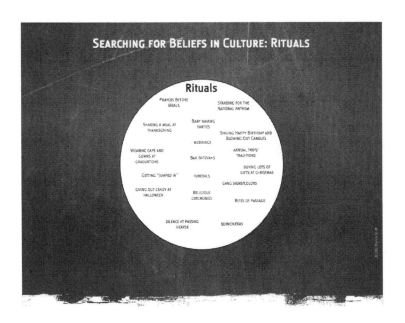

Rituals also give you a clue about your deepest values and beliefs. Rituals are collective activities in achieving a specific goal. The rituals themselves do not necessarily mean anything, but which, within a culture, are considered as socially essential. Rituals are thus carried out for their own sake. The way we pray, or don't pray, before meals. The way we stand for the National Anthem. The way was share a meal at Thanksgiving. These are all rituals. Others include baby naming parties, weddings, funerals, giving out candy on Halloween, singing happy birthday and blowing out candles are all rituals. Buying lots of gifts at Christmas or some other holiday.

When I was younger, whenever a funeral procession was driving by with a hearse leading the way, my family and I always stopped, removed our hates, and "paid our respects." When someone died, even if it was a stranger, there was a reverence that we were taught to have at passing hearses. That ritual reflected a much deeper value and belief about life and death.

What are some of your rituals? What do those rituals mean? Why do you do them? What do they reveal about your deepest values and beliefs?

VALUES

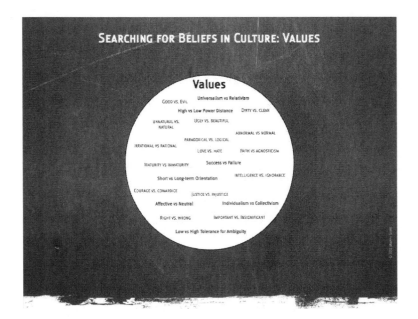

Now we move on to the next concentric circle of values. What are values? Values are broad tendencies to prefer certain states of affairs over others. Values are feelings that have a plus or minus side attached to them. They deal with: evil versus good, dirty versus clean, ugly versus beautiful, unnatural verses natural, abnormal versus normal, paradoxical versus logical, irrational versus rational, and so on.

What is important to note about values is that each of them have different meanings depending on whom you ask. What is evil to you might be good to someone else. What's dirty to you might be clean to someone else. When I was growing up, what was considered dangerous to most people was considered fun to me and my friends. You need to understand what you mean when you refer to a particular value. What does it really mean to be "good?" The more you systematically analyze the fundamental, core values you hold dear, the more clearly you will understand what you mean when you think about them, or talk about them with others.

My professor told a story of how he and his colleagues flew to Africa to teach English to some young adults. When it was time to take a test, they had to administer several tests to accommodate the large number of students who wanted to take the test. The students who took the first test failed miserably, but the students who took all the remaining tests got all the answers right. How did that happen? Well, the teachers suspected that the students from the first test went out and started telling all the other would-be test takers what was on the test. To teach the students about the importance of not cheating, the teachers called a meeting. The head teacher asked a question to the student body, "What is cheating?" One of the students stood up and said, "Cheating is having what my brother needs and not sharing it with him." That, my friend, is exactly what I'm talking about when I talk about values. What was cheating to the American teachers was not considered cheating to the African students. In your own journey, you need to get clear about what you mean when you refer to values.

What are some of your deepest values? When you say something is "beautiful" what do you mean? What makes it beautiful? Try to get specific. What about "maturity?" What does it mean to say someone is mature? Or dirty? What is love? Why do you define it that way? You answer to those questions reveal some of your deepest values and the beliefs that undergird them.

BELIEFS

Finally, you belief system, or your philosophy of life, or your frame of reference, or your worldview, is the core of your frame of reference. Your belief system reveals you beliefs about the deepest meaning of life and assumptions about the nature of reality. All human beings have ways that they make sense of the world. Is the purpose of life to acquire individual wealth or fame? Is it to promote the reputation of the extended family? Is it to please God? Is it to be happy? Is it to live a sacrificial life for others? What about the nature of reality? Is there a God, and if so, does he know me and care about me? Is there an afterlife? Does the physical world really exist, and if so, is it orderly? Are people good or bad? Do people have free will, or is life controlled by the environment? Do evil spirits and angels exist? Is there such a thing as absolute truth? These philosophical and theological presuppositions subtly direct all other cultural values that influence the way people think, feel, and act. People are aware of some aspects of their worldview

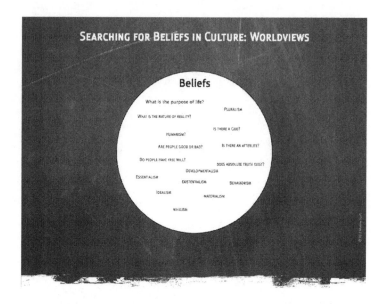

or belief system, but most assumptions are implicit.

Going forward, I would like you to pay closer attention to the symbols, heroes, and rituals in your life. When you notice something, try to understand what each one might reveal about your core values or beliefs; and, try to look for the symbols, heroes, and rituals in the lives of those yo would like to help or reach. Ask yourself, how might these things function in this persons's culture, or what might this symbolize for this person or group? I can't stress enough the importance of trying to understand before you analyze or evaluate.

I have covered all this ground about culture because I think it is imperative for you to understand that almost all expectations are culturally-based. I also want you to see how your own cultural background has influenced you. We live in a multicultural world, and I want you to do well in it. I am convinced that if you are going to reach and teach people today in our increasingly multicultural world, you must first understand your own cultural values. Understanding our own culture and our own assumptions and expectations about how people "should" think and act is the basis for success in reaching and teaching youth today.

CHAPTER 7: EXPERIENCES

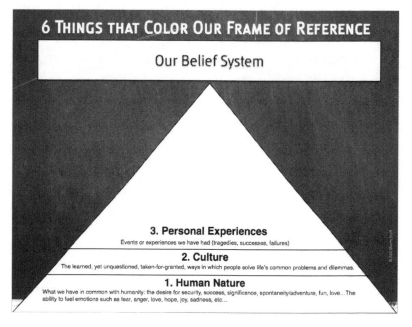

6 THINGS THAT COLOR OUR FRAME OF REFERENCE

Our Belief System

3. Personal Experiences
Events or experiences we have had (tragedies, successes, failures)

2. Culture
The learned, yet unquestioned, taken-for-granted, ways in which people solve life's common problems and dilemmas.

1. Human Nature
What we have in common with humanity: the desire for security, success, significance, spontaneity/adventure, fun, love...The ability to feel emotions such as fear, anger, love, hope, joy, sadness, etc...

Have you had any personal experiences that deeply affected your development as a person? What did it teach you, about yourself, others, about life? Have you taken a vacation or a trip that changed how you saw the world? Have you had any jobs that shaped your own personal ambitions?

I'll never forget one of my first jobs at a well known fast food restaurant where I made $4 an hour. I was a junior in high school, and I used to go to that job every day after school. I used to make the sandwiches, mop the floors, wash the dishes, clean the fry machine, and spend a considerable amount of time in the freezers checking on our products. After about three months on that job, I became really motivated to do something else with my life. I realized then, while cleaning out those dreaded fry machines that fast food work was not for me. I needed to go to college and do something that would allow me to make a living and a difference with my mind. I do not knock anyone who is working at a fast food restaurant making an honest living. I just learned that working there was not for me. Because I realized that that kind of work was not for me, I started working even harder at school. Have you had any jobs like that?

Did you grow up in a home with two parents? One parent? How did that shape your values and beliefs? While reflecting on my 12 year wedding anniversary, I realized that I don't have a reference point of what a healthy, happy marriage looks like. Other than what I have seen on The Cosby Show, I have not had a real-life example of how to build a healthy, happy marriage. I have never been close enough to a man who has been happily married. Sure, I've known a few men in my life who have been married, but I have not spent enough time with any of them to know what their marriages were really like. How do they handle disagreements? How do they resolve conflict? How do they navigate discussions about money, faith, children, family, disappointment, fear, success, etc.? Even if their marriages were/are solid, I have not had the privilege of spending enough time with them to observe how they have dealt with the challenges I have faced as a man, husband, father, or friend.

My father never married my mother, and was not around for most of my life; my first step-father and mother separated when I was five years old; my second step-father was married to my mom for under a decade. I once had a pastor who seemed like he had a good marriage, but I was barely fifteen years old, and I could not have cared less about the subject of marriage. Therefore, I am pretty sure I have I felt so strange about my anniversaries lately because I've never been here before, and nobody I have spent a considerable amount of time with has ever made it this far either. Because of that, I have been on my own, trying to find my own way; and, the road has been anything but ideal.

Given this reality, how, then, have I been able to have such a happy, healthy, and fulfilling marriage? Why are things working out so well? Shouldn't I have ruined it by now?

As I reflect on the road I've taken, it has become clear to me that a lot of who I am today as a man and husband, and how I live my life, is largely because of what I have been *running from*. For years I have been driven by the desire to be different from the men who hurt my mother during my childhood. I've been running from the examples of those men. I never wanted to be like them. Some of them partied and went to clubs all the time, so I decided that I would not party or club; some were alcoholics, so I decided that I would not drink alcohol; some were drug addicts, so I decided that I would not do drugs (Although I did go through a phase of getting drunk and smoking weed before I made the decision to turn my life around); some were verbally and mentally abusive, so I made a decision to never call women out of their names; some were physically abusive, so I made the decision to never put my hands on a woman; some cheated, so I made a decision that I would never violate my wife's trust; most of them spent very little time with their children, so I made a decision to one day love, cherish, play with, and cultivate my children. I have been running pretty hard to be a contrarian.

Upon further reflection about how I have been able to enjoy such a rich and fulfilling marriage, it has become clearer to me that it might also have something to do with what I have been *running to*. I have been running to a very particular future. For me, when I think about the final moments of my life, I have a picture in my head of what I hope those moments will be like. I hope to have my wife there. I see myself holding her hand, and looking into her eyes, one last time. I see us reminiscing about our life together. I see us smiling, one more time, at all of the great, and fun, and silly things we did to bring ourselves and others joy (Like we did on our honeymoon in New Orleans, when we danced in the hotel elevator thinking no one could see us, only to be greeted, on our way out of the hotel, by security and staff whose huge grins hinted that they had been watching our elevator routines on hidden cameras. We were so embarrassed! But we kept on dancing, even harder, giving them some dance routines that they would never forget).

I share that with you to help you see how personal experiences have a way of shaping your frame of reference. Do you have any powerful experiences that had such a huge impact on how you see the world? I am sure you have. Your experience do not have to be negative.

Maybe you have had a powerful religious experience, and it shaped the way you see people and things. Maybe you are a more loving and forgiving person because of a personal experience you have had at worship service.

My best friend's death made me appreciate life so much more. Being homeless made me much more sensitive to the needs of homeless people. Seeing my mother get abused made me decide that I would never put my hands on a woman. Seeing how drugs and alcohol really harmed many people in my family, I decided that drugs and alcohol would not be a part of my life. Those experiences really shaped me. Maybe you didn't go through the things I went though, but maybe you have experienced some things that had such a deep impact on you that they altered the course of your life. Whatever those things are, they have shaped your frame of reference.

In the same way, those things have shaped the frame of reference of the people you would like to reach. It would not hurt for you to try to learn about some of the stories of the people you serve. I can't tell you how many times I have had a teacher tell me that their lives were changed when they opened themselves up to learn about the lives of their students. Personal experiences have a way of shading how we see the world.

CHAPTER 8: PERSONALITY

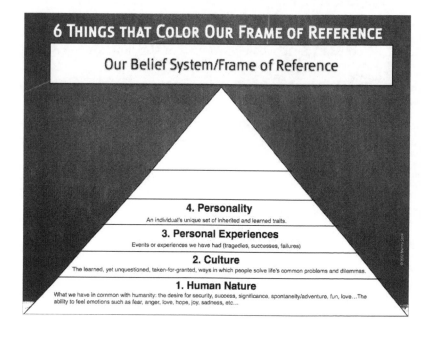

6 Things that Color Our Frame of Reference

Our Belief System/Frame of Reference

4. Personality
An individual's unique set of inherited and learned traits.

3. Personal Experiences
Events or experiences we have had (tragedies, successes, failures)

2. Culture
The learned, yet unquestioned, taken-for-granted, ways in which people solve life's common problems and dilemmas.

1. Human Nature
What we have in common with humanity: the desire for security, success, significance, spontaneity/adventure, fun, love...The ability to feel emotions such as fear, anger, love, hope, joy, sadness, etc...

In addition to being shaped by human nature, heredity, and your culture, you have also been shaped by your **personality**. Even though you share the same nature as other humans, and you share the same culture with others, your personality sets you apart from others. Your personality, though influenced by human nature, and influenced by your cultural background, is something that is unique to you.

You might be an introvert who feels drained when you're around crowds; or, you might be an extrovert who gets energized when you are around other people. You might have a dominant personality that drives you to get things done. Or you might have an influential personality, which enables you to work well with other people. Or, you might have a more precise personality, which compels you to be very meticulous with minute details. Or, you might have a very supportive personality, which leads you to prefer to work behind the scenes. No matter what your personality is, it is unique to you, and it has a great deal to do with who you are and where you are in life.

The creators of the DISC analysis have argued that there are essentially four types of personalities in the world. There is the person with the dominant personality who tends to be direct and decisive. They tend to have high self-confidence and are risk takers and problem solvers, which enables others to look to them for decisions and direction. They tend to be self-starters. Their downside is they can be argumentative and not listen to the reasoning of others. They tend to dislike repetition and routine and may ignore the details and minutia of a situation, even if it's important. They may attempt too much at one time, hoping to see quick results. Do you have a dominant personality? Dominant personalities can sometimes be abrasive and come off as harsh to people who do not understand them. I know this, because I have a dominant personality.

Then there is the influencer. Influencers are enthusiastic, optimistic, talkative, persuasive, impulsive and emotional.

They truly enjoy being around others, and function best when around people and working in teams. They tend to be great encourages and motivators of others, and they keep environments positive. Though not completely accurate, influencers tend to be more concerned with people and popularity than with tangible results and organization. Are you an influencer?

Or maybe you have a Supporter personality. People with supportive personalities are steady, stable, and predictable. They are even-tempered, friendly, sympathetic with others, and very generous with loved ones. They tend to be conscientious and are good at multi-tasking and seeing tasks through until completion

Their challenge is that they are generally opposed to change and may also hold grudges when they experience frustrations and resentments.

Or, maybe you are an anchor, someone who is accurate, precise, detail-oriented, and conscientious. They think very analytically and systematically and make decisions carefully with plenty of research and information to back it up. When something is proposed, it is the anchor who will think through every detail of how it works and the process. Anchors tend to avoid conflict rather than argue, and it is difficult to get them to verbalize their feelings. They can be bound by procedures and methods, and find it difficult to stray from order. Finally, they can get too bogged down in the small details, making it difficult to see the next steps or big picture.

If you had to pick two of the above personality types, which would you choose to best describe yourself? What would your closest friends and colleagues say about you? Would they say you have a dominant personality or more of a meticulous one? It is important to understand your own personality, because it is very possible that others misunderstand you because of it. Because I have a dominant personality, and I now know I have one because my wife and others have helped me accept this fact about myself, I realize that I need to soften things when I am talking to people who are influences, supporters, or anchors. I realize that I need to give more details when I am talking to anchors, and that I need to be less structured when talking to influencers. This kind of knowledge about myself has helped me maintain decent relationships with most people.

How might others be misunderstanding you because of your personality type? In any case, I share this with you so you can be aware of how your own personality type might be perceived by others with whom you work or serve.

What about the personalities of the people you would like to reach. Try to describe their personality-types of the people you serve. What about your co-workers? Your supervisor? Your spouse?

CHAPTER 9: EDUCATION

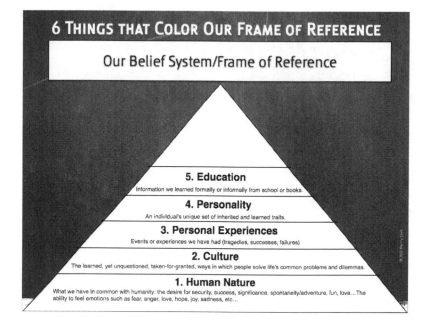

6 THINGS THAT COLOR OUR FRAME OF REFERENCE

Our Belief System/Frame of Reference

5. Education
Information we learned formally or informally from school or books.

4. Personality
An individual's unique set of inherited and learned traits.

3. Personal Experiences
Events or experiences we have had (tragedies, successes, failures)

2. Culture
The learned, yet unquestioned, taken-for-granted, ways in which people solve life's common problems and dilemmas.

1. Human Nature
What we have in common with humanity: the desire for security, success, significance, spontaneity/adventure, fun, love…The ability to feel emotions such as fear, anger, love, hope, joy, sadness, etc…

Your frame of reference has also been shaped by your education. There are two kinds of education, the kind that others give to you, and the kind that you give yourself. The first kind is the one you receive at school; the second kind is the one you get by reading books that were not assigned to you at school.

You are shaped by both kinds. I talk to many young people who say they "hate" school. They feel as though school is not related to their everyday lives. I understand how they feel, because the truth of the matter is, I used to hate school, too. I hated reading, I hated writing, and I hated math. I hated being called on in class by my teachers, because I hated being embarrassed every time I gave the wrong answer. After letting people know that I hated school, I let them know that I had to change the way I viewed school. I had to change the way I viewed books. I had to change the way I viewed math. Ultimately, I had to change the way I viewed myself.

Changing my perception was so important because I thought I wasn't as smart as the other students. They always seemed to have the right answers. They had better clothes than me, they had better things than me, and it even seemed like the teachers liked them more than me (I know for a fact some teachers did like other students more than they liked me). Even though those things were true, I had to ask myself, "If I don't take school seriously, how am I going to end up?" It didn't take me long to realize that I would end up like many people in my family who didn't take school seriously. They were working jobs that they hated, they were living in poor neighborhoods, they were living in tiny apartments, they were always fighting over money, and they always seemed miserable. Many of them were in prison, some were alcoholics, and some were addicted to drugs. I know that none of them planned on ending up that way. I also know that society makes it harder on some people than on others. However, I also made up my mind that I refused to be poor, I refused to be on drugs, I refused to be an alcoholic, I refused to live in poor neighborhoods unwillingly, and I refused to be just like a bunch of people that I had grown up around—people who drank, smoked, played dominoes, cards, and talked trash all day.

I decided that even though it would be hard, I was going to take school seriously. I began seeing books as conversations waiting to be picked up. I began to see math as a game or a puzzle that needed to be figured out. I began to see homework as an opportunity to get better as a person. I began to see school as a way out of poverty, depression, and despair. Once I made that decision, I began treating my teachers better, and began developing better relationships with the adults around me. I knew that not all of them really cared about me or my success, but I also know that there were several who genuinely cared about me, and who wanted me to be my best. I developed relationships with those teachers, and to this day, I thank them for pouring much of their lives into me.

That is the kind of education that others give to you. It's the kind that leads to diplomas, degrees, and certificates.

The second kind of education is the kind that you give to yourself. You may not get a degree for this kind of education, but it certainly makes a bigger impression on you. To give yourself an education means that you don't have a teacher, instructor, professor, parent, or some authority figure holding you accountable for the books you read, and the papers you write. You don't have any quizzes, tests, midterms, or final exams to take. This is the kind of education that requires you to buy books on topics that you are interested in. It is the kind of education that causes you to stay up through the night because you are so enthralled by the things you are learning. It is the kind of education that nobody can take away from you.

When I was in college, most of the things I learned were learned from books that were not assigned to me by my professors. I used to complete my assignments for class, and then go to the library and stay there for hours, reading books about rhetoric, argument, philosophy, English, Spanish, geography, politics, law, and society. I became a student whose thirst for wisdom and knowledge was so insatiable that I would often stay at the library until two or three in the morning, even when school was out of session. I often went to bookstores, and just looked through every section, trying to find something that could help me become a better, more knowledgeable person. To this day, I love books, and I have thousands of them that continue to inspire me, sharpen me, and equip me to make a difference in the world.

In the same way, your education has shaped your frame of reference. It has affected how you see the world. Take a moment to reflect on any teachers you have had who have changed your mind or life. Think about books you have read, or lectures you have read that had a deep impact on you. Think about speakers you have heard at professional development seminars. All of those things have shaded your frame of reference as well.

Also, think about the education of the people you serve. What kind of schools did they attend? Urban? Suburban? Rural? Title 1? What kinds of classes and teachers have they had? How might those things have shaped or shaded that person's frame of reference?

CHAPTER 10: IMAGINATION

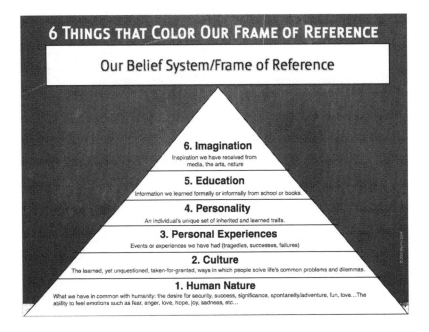

When I was still a young man in high school, when I was still learning the basics of English grammar—long before I became a public speaker—a substitute teacher in my history class put on a video of Martin Luther King's "I Have a Dream" Speech. I had never been more inspired in my life. Watching that man speak from the depths of his soul inspired by something that was beyond this world impacted me in powerful ways. While listening to him and watching him speak, I got goose bumps, and something in my heart said,

"you are supposed to do something like that with your life."
From that moment, I have never been the same.

From that moment, I began seeing visions of myself
standing before large groups of people, inspiring them with
words that I was speaking. Sometimes, when I heard other
speakers make presentations during assemblies, I often saw
myself delivering my own message in their place.

The same thing happened to me in college, at the
University of California at Berkeley. Because of these visions
of myself speaking to large crowds, I often mentally
transformed my little bedroom into a coliseum where an old
upright speaker became my lectern, and all the objects in my
room became my audience. For hours I would recite poetry
and speeches in my empty room.

During college, I worked for pennies as a Loss Prevention
Specialist—just a fancy name for security guard. It was my
job to secure the buildings by making sure all the doors were
locked, the lights were off, and the place was empty. Many
nights, after all the buildings were secure, I went to the largest
ballroom in the building (Pauley Ballroom), and for hours, I
recited speeches to an empty room. Eventually, I found myself
doing that in the largest venues on campus (such as Wheeler
Auditorium), which sat over seven hundred people. I even
found a way to practice a few times on the platform of the
eighty-five-hundred-seat Hearst Greek Theater. Even though
each venue was empty, in my mind, I was speaking to a

standing-room only crowd of people who were being inspired by my words. I would speak as though the room were packed to capacity with people who needed to hear what I had to say. I would speak, inspiring thousands, painting for them a vision of a brighter tomorrow. I would speak, telling people that in spite of where they come from, they can achieve their dreams. I would speak, and I would see, in my head, lives being changed.

Mentally, emotionally, and behaviorally I was committed to making that dream a reality, and it all started with my imagination being inspired. Because of a video of a man speaking, I was inspired to start reading books about speaking, and studying some of the world's most powerful speakers. When I went to sleep, I had dreams about speaking, and, in my dreams, I saw lives being changed. I saw people being moved by my words. You could not tell me that those dreams were not real, because everything about them affected my body physically. Sometimes I would wake up from those dreams and I would be sweating. Sometimes my heart would be racing. In those dreams, I had conversations with my role models. In my dreams, I remember walking around with the Rev. Dr. Martin Luther King Jr. I would watch him, and listen to him, and learn from him … in my dreams. I saw Frederick Douglass, and others, close up, in my dreams. I saw myself speaking before audiences, in my dreams. As I write these words, my heart is beginning to speed up, because I remember those dreams so vividly.

Around that time, people began to invite me to be the master of ceremonies for campus events. I became the guy who was on the microphone engaging, entertaining, and empowering audiences, young and old. Shortly after that, I began receiving invitations to speak to elementary and middle school students. Then I began receiving invitations to speak to high school students. Before long, I began receiving invitations to speak to community organizations. Eventually, I began receiving invitations to speak in other states. Finally, I began to receive invitations to speak in other countries.

I share this story with you to help you see the power of the imagination. Our imaginations have the power to shape our frame of reference so much that the control what we see and how we see it.

Do you have any inspirational encounters that have shaped your life? Any dreams, stories, movies, songs, performances, paintings, sights in nature? Think about it, because imagination, too, shades and colors our frame of reference.

What about the imaginations of your students? What movies, books, stories, or songs have shaped their imaginations about the world?

CHAPTER 11: BELIEFS

I have spent all this time talking about culture, personal experiences, personality, education, and imagination because I need you to see how your belief system or frame of reference was shaped; and, I wanted you to understand that your frame of reference determines <u>what you see</u> and <u>how you see it</u>. As such, regardless of who you <u>think</u> you see or what you see, it's important for you to take a look at yourself. This is important, because if there is anything *in you* that might be getting in the way of reaching underperforming, despondent, troubled, fragile young people, then the first thing you need to do is acknowledge those things, and then work to remove them.

What are some of those things that you might need to recognize or remove? The first thing you need to remove is your pride. If there is anything in your past, any accomplishment, any accolade, any cultural value, any superlatives, any trophies, or championships–really, anything that could make you feel like you are inherently a better person than others- you need to remove that immediately!

In place of your pride, you need to take an honest assessment of yourself, and realize that you are not much different from, or better than, the young person that you are trying to reach. Yes, your circumstances may be much better than the person you're trying to reach, but your circumstances do not make you inherently a better person than the person you're trying to reach. You need to look at the person that you're trying to help as someone who is not much different from you. You need to see them as human beings. You need to see them as someone who has dreams just like you. You need to see them as someone who has hopes and aspirations, just like you. The specifics of their dreams and their ambitions may be very different from yours, but at the core of their being, they have something—or they had something—that used to motivate them or inspire them.

You need to understand that if you had been given the circumstances that that person you're trying to reach has been given, chances are you would be in same situation as that young person. So, the first thing you need to do is to understand that the young person you are trying to reach is just like you.

That person hurts just like you. That person may be going through a phase just like you did at that age. That person may be experiencing something at home that is traumatizing him or her just like you did. The first thing you want to do is try to understand that this is a human being- that he or she is someone who is valuable and significant; that he or she, at a different point or time, with a different set of circumstances, would have probably turned out just like you.

Sometimes I hear conversations about nature versus nurture–about whether one's behavior is determined by one's biology or by one's circumstances. I am convinced it is a both-and answer. I believe we are shaped by our biology and our environment. If that is the case, then you need to recognize that the young person that you are trying to reach has been given a certain set of circumstances that have influenced them to make certain kinds of decisions, which, in turn, have put them in the situation that they are in.

All this is to say, never allow yourself to become the kind of person who feels that you are better than other people, period. Never allow yourself to become the kind of person who has to boast about all of your accomplishments in order to make yourself feel better than other people. If you find yourself constantly talking to others about your accomplishments, then chances are, you have some pride in your heart that you need to address. One of my favorite proverbs says, "like clouds and winds without rain is a man who boasts of gifts he doesn't have." A person who boasts, in other words, if someone who is empty. That is to say, those who boast are all air. Don't allow yourself to become that kind of person. Let your speech be filled with grace, with love, with positivity. Let your conversation be seasoned with humility.

CHAPTER 12: RACE

After I spoke to a group of high school students in a small, homogenous town whose citizens were predominantly of European-descent, a young woman sent me a message that described her prejudices against me before hearing me speak. She said, "I was sitting in a classroom a few days ago waiting to fall asleep as some black guy- a stranger- was preparing to talk to a group of [white] high school students. I was thinking ahead to what your sob story would be, what a waste time your speech would be, how you would not be able to relate to us on "our level," and how soon it would hopefully be over with." She eventually went on to apologize for her wrong "assumptions" about me, and thanked me for giving her a new perspective about "black people," for giving her hope, and inspiration to improve her own life.

That was not the first time I have heard such sentiments being expressed. In fact, that young woman's ideas are probably more common than one would like to believe. But how did she get those ideas about black people? What would lead her to think that the color of my skin would determine the content of my speech, my intellectual capacity, and my qualifications as a speaker?

More specifically, I wondered, how did people of African descent, or "black people," come to be seen as ignorant, indolent, governed by caprice, intellectually inferior, and devoid of civility? I started doing some research, and learned some that I hope can help you become a better servant-leader in this multi-cultural world.

The idea that one's biology and behavior is predetermined by one's race has a very interesting, and complex, history. In his book, _Race: The History of an Idea in the West_, Ivan Hannaford meticulously argues that race as an organizing idea- a lens through which much of the world is seen today- was "remarkably absent" in the ancient world. He says the seed of the idea of race did not emerge until the 13th to 16th centuries. However, it was not until the 17th century that the idea of race was legitimized by the scientific community. The unexamined ethnocentricity through which European and American scientists saw ethnic "others" skewed their analysis and their conclusions, thus reinforcing the ideological racism that had been laid in previous centuries.

With the scientific authority behind them, Europeans saw race as a means by which to justify the exclusion, oppression, colonization, and the eventual enslavement of ethnic others. In fact, scholars have pointed out that the very idea of race emerged as an informal ideology that legitimated slavery and oppression of African and indigenous people.

It was in Jamestown, Massachusetts that we catch a glimpse of the nascent stages of race in the United States. When the British began to settle in the New World, and sought to make profit, they initially hired indentured servants from

Europe to work the land. However, because those Europeans knew the language and the looks, they could escape, and blend in with people who had settled in other colonies, the British quickly realized that they needed another plan.

At that point, the British turned to Native Americans, making them into indentured servants. However, because Native Americans could survive on the terrain quite well, they, like their European predecessors, escaped and returned to their families.

With no labor force in place, and with the trans-Atlantic slave trade becoming increasingly efficient, the British decided to purchase African slaves. Because the slaves did not know the language of the settlers, they did not share the same culture, and they did not look anything like the British settlers, African slaves had a much harder time trying to escape. They could not blend in with other settlers. Therefore, Africans were deemed the perfect solution to the British problem regarding labor.

The British became so dependent on those African slaves that they created categories to make their arrangements permanent. explains that "This preference for African labor was institutionalized in custom and law. Within thirty years of Jamestown's founding, color terms began to appear in colony legislation. For example, "negro" servants could be held for life, but not "whites." The idea of race, or color, then, came into being in order to subjugate African slaves, and make sure that their enslavement ended in death only.

With these arrangements in place, race became a marker, a banner, for social status. What those in power did not realize is that the meanings they imputed to race were a mirror of the political and social realities that they had created. Of course, because Africans, and people of African descent were denied the opportunities to get educations and develop culturally, it would make sense that they could not read, write, or excel in other, more culturally refined, areas. Their realities were the consequence of the social and political conditions under which they lived, not their biological make-ups. Blind to their own ethnocentricity, the British equated "black" as someone who was inferior, undeserving of rights, and incapable of being civilized. Black symbolized savagery, ignorance, lack of intelligence, and an inability to live in a civilized manner.

Although almost no scientist, or anthropologist today would argue that race, as we have described it, exists ontologically, the consequences of such ideology pervades the world today, and shapes what we see and how we see it. The fact that a young girl of European descent would question my legitimacy as a speaker, and question my intellectual capacity, because I *appear to be* of African descent is a remnant of centuries of systemic racism.

Although I have lived in a very racialized world my entire life, I have never really thought very critically about it. I had never taken the time to study the history of the idea, and how it developed over the years. I always assumed that race was somehow real, and that it somehow helped us to understand people better. But from my own experiences, augmented by my studies, I have come to see that ethnicity, especially as it relates to skin color, and other markers, is quite difficult to understand. However, because race is so deeply ingrained in our understanding of ourselves and the world around us, one would do well to think about it more carefully. Indeed, a major work of deconstruction and reconstruction becomes an inescapable must for us if reach people effectively in this day and age.

PART 2: R.E.A.C.H.

Up to this point in the book, I have been slowly laying the foundation for reaching others. For years, I used to jump right into my approach to reaching others without ever really discussing frame of reference. However, I realized that long before we begin reaching others, we need to take a careful look at ourselves to see what expectations and biases we might be bringing to the situation.

Now, we turn to my R.E.A.C.H. approach to reaching people who seem unreachable.

CHAPTER 13: RELATIONSHIPS

Let us go back to the point in my story that I began sharing with you in the first chapter of this book. Do you remember that young man- the younger, troubled version of me - who was sitting on a park bench? The young man who had just dropped out of high school and who was probably going to do something that resulted in him getting locked up or killed- do you remember him? That was me. It was really me. No exaggeration. I was in a very dark situation. Now imagine you are walking by that young man on that park bench. What do you think needed to be done first in order for someone to reach me, and others like the younger me?

I am absolutely convinced that the very first thing you need to do to reach young people is strive to build a relationship with them. Without a healthy relationship, you will limit your effectiveness as a leader or a teacher. The maxim is true, people do not care how much you know, until they know how much you care. You show you care by building a healthy relationship.

My eleventh-grade English teacher, Erin Gruwell, who came from an upper-middle class family, came into my classroom full of students Blacks, Latinos, Asians, and several Caucasian students. Culturally and socioeconomically, she was worlds apart from us, and yet she was still able to reach most of us because she knew how to build relationships with us.

If you want to work well cross-culturally, the most important thing is not technical skills. Rather, they said, you need to know how to make a friend. You need to know how to build relationships. You need to know how to enter into someone's life, so that they can learn to trust you, and so you can be an encouragement and a help to them. I'm going to share with you what I call the road to real relationships.

OPENNESS

I think we start off in life with an openness toward life. We are open to new people, and open to new experiences, and open to the adventure that life has to offer. But then life happens, and begins to make us close ourselves off from the world around us. Maybe we get our feelings hurt, or someone bullies us at school, or someone attacks our character, or talks about us behind our back. Maybe someone complained about something you said or did. Or, maybe you received a bad job review, or lost a job, or made a mistake that harmed your reputation. Whatever it is, there is a tendency among many people to cross their arms, and close themselves off from being open, vulnerable, or receptive to things and people that are new and different.

However, the people that changed my life are those who embodied openness in the best way. My former professor, Dr.

Duane Elmer once said, "Openness is the ability to welcome people into your presence so that they feel safe and secure." The word hospitality it has same root as the word hospital, and when you go to a hospital, what are you looking for? You're looking to be made well; you're looking for healing. In the same way, I believe when you extend hospitality to someone, you help them heal.

Openness is the ability to have a posture about you, to have a demeanor about you, that makes others feel safe and secure. When you embody openness, your eyes smile when you see someone. When people come into your presence, your warmth lifts their spirits. People feel safe and secure when they can see, in your eyes, that you are happy to see them.

I had teachers come into my life, who, when when I walked into their presence, they were so open, so loving, and so welcoming that I enjoyed being around them. Whenever I got close to them, they would greet me with such warmth and kindness. They greeted me in such a way that I sometimes felt myself begin heal emotionally.

It was weird. Something inside me began to heal by the way these people treated me, by the way they welcomed me into their presence. When I walked into their classrooms, they were happy to see me. When I walked into their offices, they were there to greet me with a warm smile, a pat on the back, and a smile in their eyes.

I met a teacher in Columbia, South Carolina who said that she had been having problems with the lunch lady of the school, but did not know why. After talking to the lunch lady and a few trusted friends, and she concluded that the was coming off as a rude and mean person, even though she was not aware of it. She identified herself as an introvert, and realized that others perceived her introversion as rude, distant, and unfriendly. That epiphany to her forced her to work on becoming more open to others.

Do you come off as open to others? Or, do you come off as someone who is rude, abrasive, or cold? It would not hurt (well, maybe a little) to ask some people whose opinion you value, and hear what they have to say about their perceptions of you. Their revelations might help you to grow.

Another teacher I met recently told me that she had been feeling down, drained, and depressed. She said that it was sapping her of her joy, and robbing her of her motivation to teach. Then one day she decided that she was going change her attitude about her job. She said that she decided that she was going to greet each day with love in her heart, and gratitude for the little things. That little shift altered everything for her. She said she now walks onto campus more open, enthusiastic, and ready to learn and teach.

Dr. Robert Long, a pastor in Oklahoma City is a perfect example of what it means to embody openness. I did an internship at his church several years ago, and spent a good deal of time with Dr. Long. Whenever I saw in person, or talked with him on the phone, he greeted me in the most enthusiastic, spirit-lifting way. He would say, with the biggest smile on his face, and a joy in his eyes, "MANNY!!!!" No matter how low I might have been feeling, his presence always had a way of bringing me joy.

What about you? Can you welcome someone into your presence with an openness so that they feel secure, safe, and uplifting? Do you greet people in a way that they feel that they do not have to watch their backs, or so they do not feel like that they need to worry that you might hurt them? To be sure, I am not saying you need to have unbridled enthusiasm and contagious optimism (even those things are not bad). All I am recommending is that you work on greeting each day and each person with more openness.

I'll be the first to admit that embodying openness is not always an easy thing to do. Sometimes with all of the administrative work that you have to do, and the lesson plans that you need to prepare; with all the demands on your time...it is hard to be open.

Sometimes we are just too busy. The problem with being too busy, however, is that it causes you close yourself off from other people. Busy-ness prevents you from embodying openness.

But because openness is a prerequisite to reaching anyone, you <u>must</u> work on becoming less busy. You must manage your time more carefully. Do whatever you need to do become more emotionally and mentally available to new people, information, and situations. This is fundamental. It is an inescapable must for you to develop.

ACCEPTANCE

In addition to openness, I highly recommend you work develop acceptance, or tolerance for others. Now let me be clear- by acceptance I do not mean you need to accept and celebrate everyone's choices and lifestyles. That is not want I'm saying. In fact, I think that kind of acceptance is un-livable and disingenuous. By acceptance I am referring the ability to continue seeing beauty, potential, value, and worth, even though you see their "issues." It means being able to continue holding someone in high regard even though you see their low estate. It's your ability to continue venerating someone even though you see their issues; it's the ability to continue seeing potential even though you see a lot of problems. I'll admit to you that it is very hard to embody acceptance.

Where I'm from, having lived in thirty-eight places, I've learned that most people love you until they know you. People will love you when you are dressed up, and you are paying for their meals. They love you when you agree with them. They love you when you meet their standards. However, when people see the imperfect parts of you- your character flaws, and your brokenness, and your bad attitude, or your insecurity, and your shortcoming- they usually distance themselves from you. More often than not, when people see your issues, they stop loving you. They love you until they know you, but once they know you- more often than not-they stop loving you.

However, those who have changed my life are those who saw my issues and insecurities and inadequacies, but did not give up on me. They did not act as though my issues were invisible, or that they did not exist. Rather, they saw my issues, but they also saw *past* my issues. They looked past my issues and saw something greater. They saw that I did not know how to study, but they also saw a college graduate. They noticed that I had a bad temper, but they also saw someone who could one day have peace. They someone who had several character flaws, and they also saw someone who could achieve great things. They saw my problems, but did not hold them against me. Instead, they saw my potential, and kept calling me up to it. They accepted me.

Acceptance is key if you're going to reach anyone. If you're going to build a relationship with anyone, you have to work to focus on their potential, even though you see their problems. It is the ability to continue venerating someone when you could just as well vilify them. It's the ability to see someone's worth even though you have a whole lot of reasons to see what's wrong. It's the ability to continue loving someone even though they may not have done anything to really deserve it. Can you love someone whose behavior you do not like? Can you accept someone who has bad habits? When that young person comes into your classroom with a bad attitude, and doesn't want to talk to you, can you still see worth? Can you accept the young person who has his head down on his desk- the one who didn't do his homework, who maybe got into a fight the day before?

A kindergarten teacher told me a story of one of her kids who had a lot of issues. One morning, when she greeted him as he walked into class, he lashed out at her, saying, "You're ugly, you're stupid, and you're fat." She responded, saying, "Sounds like somebody needs a hug! Come here!" And she commenced to squeeze him. That's what acceptance looks like.

My friend, practicing acceptance, or tolerance, is not easy to do. But let me just free you up just in case you don't know this- the person wearing your clothes right now, reading these words right now, has some issues. Sorry to burst your bubble, but we all have some issues. We all have some shortcomings. We all have some character flaws.

So, with your issues, can you give the people you work with permission to have issues? Can you give the young people you work with permission to have issues? Can you give them permission to have some brokenness in their lives? Can you give your colleagues permission to be imperfect? What about your supervisor? Can they have issues? The better you are able to embody acceptance, the better your chances of reaching them will be.

Your practicing of acceptance will open so many doors for you. Loving others when they feel unloveable will break down so many barriers for you. Your acceptance, your love for them, will surprise them. It will shock them. They'll wonder, "Why is this person treating me this way?" "Why are they still nice to me even though I've done everything in my power to get this person out of my face?" "Why does this person still go out of his way to let me know that he cares about me?" "Why does this person keep encouraging me, even though I have not demonstrated that I am willing to work hard? Why?"

The more you practice acceptance, the less others will understand why you are still working with them- which is exactly what you want. Your love for them allows you to say, "Yes, I see your brokenness. Yes, I see your shortcomings. Yes, I see your character flaws. Yes, I know your mama said you weren't going to be anybody. But I see something great in you. Yes, I know your father has been gone, and you do not know what it means to be a man? Yes, I know that you have been irresponsible. But I still love you and believe in you. Yes, I understand that some things happened to you in your life that hurt you; but, I still see a high school graduate. I see a doctor. I see a lawyer. I see a teacher. I still see someone who can be happily married. I see someone who can one day be a great father, or mother. I see someone who can make a big difference in this world." That's what acceptance looks and sounds like in real life. When you speak those things into the lives of young people who are living beneath their potential, you will be well on your way to building a great relationship with them.

TRUST

I have felt betrayed or abandoned so many times in my life that my heart became so sore that it could not bear the touch of being hurt by anyone else. To protect myself, I put up emotional walls to keep people from getting close to me. I let them get close enough to feel connected, but not so close that they could hurt me. In order to get me to let down my walls, several people had to get me to trust them.

To build a healthy relationship with the people you want to reach, you need to learn how to develop trust. Trust is the ability to build confidence in the relationships so that both parties believe the other will not intentionally injure them, but, in fact, act in the other's best interest.

The foundation of every relationship is trust. If you do not have trust, if you can't earn someone's trust, they will never allow you to get close enough to them to reach them. They will never allow you to speak things into their lives because they will always question your motives. They'll always question your agenda. Trust is the ability to make someone feel as though you you really care about them, and that you want what is best for them, and not just what's best for you.

I met a teacher who baked one of her students a birthday cake for his birthday, and gave it to him. Surprised, he thanked her, and walked away with his cake. The next day, she saw him at his locker, and in his locker was the birthday cake she had given him. It was uneaten. He hadn't touched it. Surprised, she asked him why he hadn't eaten it. He told her that no one had ever given him a birthday cake, and he didn't want to ruin it. That teacher's little act of generosity went a long way with that student.

I met another teacher who was about seventy years old, and who had an amazing impact on his kids. When I asked him to reveal his secret to me, he said that he picked one or two students a day to privately encourage. He wrote them little notes, and gave them little gifts, or spent a little extra time speaking encouraging words to them. He told me, "Manny, I don't know how much longer I have to live. My wife died recently, and I don't know how much longer I got. But with the time I have left, I just want these kids to know that I care about them, that they matter to me, that I love them." The kids loved that man. They trusted him. It was a beautiful thing to see. His little acts of kindness had a big impact on his kids, and on me. His kids were white, latino, black, and Asian; they were rich and poor; and, they all loved him.

What are some things you can do to build that kind of trust in your relationships? It won't happen by accident. You have to be intentional about it.

LEARNING

Next on the road to developing real relationships is learning. If people trust you, you can then begin learning things about them, learning from them, and learning with them. Those are at least three levels of learning. When you walk into a into a classroom of strangers, and you're the teacher, it is your job to influence them. It's your job to affect change in their lives. As such, you would do well to become students of that group of people. You would do well to become an anthropologist of them and their cultures. I spent a great deal of time in the first part of the book talking about frame of reference, so I will not spend much more time here talking about the things you need to learn.

All I will say is that you would do well to find out whom your students emulate. You would do well to learn about their music. Who are their role models? Who do they look up to? Why do they dress that way? How do they dress, why are they wearing those pants? Why are some wearing Cortez Nikes? Why are some wearing Dickies? Why are some sagging their pants? Why are some wearing extra large white T-shirts? Why are some wearing wave caps? Why are some wearing gold teeth and silver teeth in their mouths? Why do they have tattoos, and what do they mean? What are they trying to tell you about who they are, and how they see themselves, and what they value? What music are they listening to? What are they internalizing? What are they are imbibing? What are they reading? Which magazines? Which websites are they visiting? What are they posting on Facebook? On Twitter? Instagram? What about Pinterest? Snapchat?

All that is to ask, what can you do to learn about your students from afar? Become a student of your students, so you can learn much more about them.

Trust me, studying your students will be very useful for you when I discuss engagement in the next chapter.

But right now, you need to learn about them from afar. Just observe them. They wont let you in at first, but if you have this attitude of openness and acceptance and you're developing trust; and, you are going out of your way to invest in this relationship, then you can learn about them.

Then, eventually you'll learn from them. They'll tell you things that they normally don't tell adults. They'll start sharing confidential things with you. You'll start learning more deeply, more carefully, more personally about these young people.

There's a story of some young ladies I think they were in Florida, I do not remember the state, but they were wearing all of these colorful shoestrings. Eventually, a teacher was able to earn the trust of one of the young ladies in her school, and the teacher asked about the meaning of the girls wearing colorful shoestrings. Was it just a fad? Or was there something more going on? The teacher found out that the shoestrings were really a menu to let them know what the girls were willing to do sexually.

The teacher was blown away, and eventually that teacher had to share that information with the leadership of the school. What do you think the school district did? No more colorful shoestrings! No more colorful shoestrings! What do you think the young ladies, the girls, did? Initially, they complied. However, a little bit later, after the paranoia had died down, the girls started wearing little bracelets and wristbands, and they began communicating another way. You see, young people today and young people in every generation, speak another language. It's almost like the dog whistle- when humans blow a dog whistle we as human beings can't hear it; but the dogs can hear it quite well. Now I am not saying that children are dogs; my point is simply that they have another language.

Is it possible that the young people around you are speaking another language that you can't hear, right now? Is it possible that they are communicating to one another- communicating values and their visions and things that are important to them that we can't hear? Through their clothes and through their tattoos and through their piercings and through their music and through their art and through their poetry, they are communicating; and, you will only learn what they are saying if you become students of them.

Establishing rapport with them, learning about them and then learning from them are the first two levels of learning. Eventually you will learn _with_ them. That is the third level. My best teachers learned about their students and observed us from afar. Eventually, some of us started letting them in. They started learning from us. Then, something special happened: we began learning from one another and with one another. We learned from her, and she learned from us. We learned together.

If you stop learning today, you should stop leading tomorrow. You might as well quit, because you will eventually become irrelevant. You will lose influence, and you will become outdated. Some of your techniques and methodologies will no longer be relevant to kids today.

I speak to about 150 groups a year. I have been doing this for the last 15 years, and you better believe I've worked hard to learn how to engage them. I've learned, and I'm learning how to meet people on their levels. There are times when I feel as though I am getting out of touch with some of my audiences. To correct this, I take off my teacher hat and become a student again. Staying close to the people I am trying to reach has taught me so much about myself and them. In fact, a lot of what I know has just come from me learning about them from afar, learning from them up close, and learning with them, together.

Fortunately, I've made a lot of great connections with young people. Many of them trust me and share things with me that they don't even share with their best friends. I'd like to think that they do so because I've humbled myself to learn about them, and I constantly do my best to let them know I care.

UNDERSTANDING

If you want to develop a real relationship with someone, you will eventually need to get to a place of understanding. If you are open and accepting; if you're developing trust and learning about, from, and with them, eventually you will begin to understand them. But what is understanding? It is simply the ability to see patterns of behavior and the underlying values that reveal the integrated wholeness and integrity of a person and a people. In other words, understanding gives you a sense of the tapestry of a group of people. It gives you a sense of their pulsating core. It gives you a sense of their values. Where I'm from, there were some things that were central to who we were, and how we saw ourselves. In the inner-city of Long Beach, there are some things that are common sense to me, but rather uncommon for others who are not from Long Beach.

In every city, there are some things that are unspoken rules. Insiders know them; outsiders don't. There are certain ways you carry yourself when you go in certain neighborhoods. There are certain things you talk about, and certain things you don't. That kind of knowledge comes only when you achieve understanding.

How well do you understand the young people with whom you work? Why do they talk about certain things in a certain way? Why are they reticent about other topics? Gaining an understanding about who they relate to, and why they like certain music, like hip-hop, or any genre of music, is crucial to reaching them.

Why does heavy-metal connect with a certain demographic of students?

To be sure, some of it is obvious. Other facts, not so much. The more you work to understand, the more effective you will become at building a real relationship with youth.

COMPETENCE

I think you also need some kind of competence. Competence s the ability to conduct a task well, and have other's believe in your ability to conduct a task well. There are two types of competences: there is competence by power and there is competence by information. Competence by power simply says, "I have the title, I was assigned, I am in charge, someone appointed me, I'm the boss and people will follow me because I'm in charge." People may follow you because you have the title, but they will never respect you as a person. If you only have competence by power, once you leave the room, your influence goes with you. They talk about you behind your back.

Then there is competence by information. Competence by information is when people respect you because you have information that is relevant to them. When you have this kind of competence, your persuasive capital grows tremendously.

In other words, you know some things and can do some things that can help others.

You become competent when you can do something that others need done, or have insight that others lack.

Many leaders fail to connect with young people because they lean too much on their title. It is not until youth see you have competence by information that you will have a shot at reaching them.

COMMONALITY

Another key characteristic on the road to developing real relationships is commonality. Commonality is just another way of saying you have to have the ability to give the person with whom you are speaking the perception that you want the same things; that you have a common goal. If you want to develop a real healthy, meaningful relationship with someone, you need to have a mutual trust, and you have to believe that you have a common goal- that you both want the same things.

As a leader there is nothing wrong with you pulling aside an underperforming young person and saying, "Hey, what is going on? You okay? What's's the problem?" Regardless of what they say, it is helpful to just let them know, "Look, I'm on your team. I got your back. I want you to do well. You don't have to fight me. You don't. I'm on your team, I want the same things you want. I want you to be happy. I want you to be successful. I want you to go and do great things. I want you to be fulfilled. We want the same things." When someone connects with you like that, it makes a difference. It makes a big difference.

I will never forget when a close friend of mine was given an opportunity to give himself a grade in a class, and he gave himself an F. My teacher pulled him aside, and did exactly what I mentioned above, except with a little more fire, and a few more words I dare not include here. She challenged him, and let him know that she was on his team. It made such a difference in him that he went on to become a very influential person on campus. All of us guys wanted to be just like him.

When a young person hears you say things like, "Other people may have given up on you, but I have not given up on you. I want the same things you want. I want you to be happy, but you got to work with me." When you do things like that, it can go a long way with youth.

Young people often thank me for the little time I give them after my speeches. I was recently in Texas when a line of 800 or 900 people waited to speak with me. It took me over two hours to speak to everyone. I finished my presentation at 2:45 in the afternoon, but I did not leave the school until 6 PM. As is often the case, these young people share some of the deepest secrets with me, and some of their greatest problems. They often ask me for advice about something going on in their lives.

I have found it extremely helpful to make sure people know that I want the best for them. If I sense some resistance to what I am saying to a young person, I stop and say, "Hey, I get nothing out of this. I want you to be happy. I want you to be successful. Now hear me out. I'm on your team." They often soften up a little after that, and realize that I do not personally benefit from what I'm telling them. Young people listen a little better when they believe the advice is coming from a neutral, objective, and loving place.

CHARISMA

It would help if you also have, or develop charisma. Charisma is the ability to inspire people with information that solves their major problems. For example, you might go into a community that is experiencing some kind of a major problem. Maybe it is a recession. Maybe it is high unemployment. Or maybe there is a drought. Maybe there is a high dropout rate or a high teen-pregnancy rate. Whatever the case, whenever you go into a place where people are distressed, hurting, and discouraged, those people are searching for answers. Many of them are scraping their existence for hope, and it is in that context that a leader often emerges. Someone rises up and shares a vision that he or she believes can solve their problem(s). That leader shares her heart, shares her strategy, shares her mission and, if the people believe in the vision, the people galvanize around it. They support the person with the vision and plan to help them.

In the same way, if you are going to be an effective change agent who reaches young people, you must somehow study, and understand, their problems. Only then should you begin developing solutions that meet their needs. The first part of solving any problem is understanding that problem in depth. Then, once you think you have a sense of the root causes of the problem, you can begin thinking through how to propose your solution to that problem.

As a leader with charisma, and a clear vision for young people, you will be able to speak to this younger generation with a conviction and with an authority that I believe they'll respond to. When I stand before many people who are obviously discouraged, one of my most important jobs is to help them see that there is a solution to their problems.

DYNAMISM

If you want to cultivate a real relationship with young people, you would do well to develop some kind of dynamism. Now what do I mean? Dynamism is simply your ability to be enthusiastic and passionate and personally involved in what you say and do. If I stood up in packed auditoriums of 1000, 3000, 5000 students, walked to the microphone, and started speaking in a very mellow, calm, monotone way, they would probably tune me out immediately.

My friend, if I did that, I would be out of business. Fortunately, I'm passionate about the lives of young people. I'm passionate about saving lives. It really breaks my heart when a young person, or anyone, commits suicide. It really bothers me that millions of our young people are depressed. It breaks my heart when I hear that a young person has been molested or raped. I get upset every time I hear that a young person has dropped out of high school.

Therefore, when I am scheduled to speak anywhere, I realize I may only have one chance- I only have one chance to change a life; only have one chance to give someone hope; and, only have one chance to let someone know that they are here for a reason.

I cannot afford to go in there and be really calm and mellow. I must enter that speaking engagement with dynamism, regardless of what I might be going through in my own personal life. Regardless of how I feel. I have to walk into those rooms and radiate that "today is the day! Today is the day that your life can get better. Today is the day that you can turn things around. You can't go through life waiting for someone to turn your life around! You do it for yourself! Now! Right now!"

To have dynamism means you have to be physically and emotionally invested in what you're saying.

Are you fired up about the stuff you talk about? Are you fired up because you care about these kids, and because you want to change their lives, and because you want them to make the most of their lives? Are you fired up? Because if you're going to reach them, you need to be willing to talk with enthusiasm. You need to be willing to use gestures, and stand on chairs, or jump around, or spin in circles, and whatever else might work. Now, of course, that might not be a good idea if you are dealing with emotionally neutral, low-context students.

You must be willing to step out of your comfort zone and do something that shows your heart. If you are dealing with emotionally affective, high-context youth, you've got to do something that they can feel. You have to do something that lets them know that you are passionate about what you are saying.

Yes, some might laugh. Maybe doing those kinds of things makes you uncomfortable. But again, if you want to reach them, please be willing to step out of your comfort zone. Try something that might be a little off the box. By the way, what is "the box?" Who created it? I don't even like the box? Get excited. Even if you're an introvert, there is a way for you to be invested in, and enthusiastic about, your work with youth. There is a way for you to share your passion without having to holler. You do not have to scream but you have to somehow convey you are fully invested in what you are saying.

I recently watched Steven Spielberg's movie, Lincoln. That is one of the best movies I have seen in a long time. In the movie, President Lincoln did not speak very loudly. He did not holler very often, but when he did speak, he spoke with passion. He spoke with dynamism. He spoke with a certain enthusiasm. He spoke with a certain sincerity. He spoke with a certain authenticity that connected with me, and I believe connected with the nation. That man (or least Daniel Day Lewis's portrayal of him) touched people's lives without really raising his voice.

He didn't have a strong voice, and I do not have the strongest voice. However, I do have a deep commitment to change people's lives. I believe you have that same commitment. But don't be afraid to share your heart. To let your heart influence your demeanor or words. If it is real, do not be afraid to cry sometimes. Don't be afraid to raise your voice. Don't be afraid to do something that's drastic. Don't be afraid to do something that gets their attention. Trust me, I am living proof that these things can help establish rapport with students. To be sure, I sometimes have gone too far in word or deed with some of my audiences. I was in the moment, and decided to take a risk, and it did not quite go over the way I intended. Even though things didn't go as planned, I have learned more from my mistakes than my failures. I have learned what not to do again, or learned how to do something more effectively, or differently. Your demonstrative attempts might not always go over very well, but keep trying them. You will learn about your own strengths and weaknesses, and discover some things that you might actually enjoy, and actually work.

SERVING

The last step on the journey to real relationships is serving. The first nine attributes were leading to this point. The first nine characteristics were really preparing you to get to this point. Everything we do as page turners, everything we do as leaders- as servant leaders, is to serve the people that we work with, and those we work for. Not in a slavish kind of way, but in a way that changes their lives and empowers them to turn the page.

Here is what I mean by serving. Serving is the ability to relate to people in such a way that their dignity as human beings is affirmed and they are empowered to flourish.

In other words, serving affirms people, treats people with dignity and it empowers them to turn the page. Serving helps them write new, more fulfilling chapters in their lives. If you serve someone, you're affirming them in such a way that they can flourish as human beings.

One of my mentors says, "you cannot serve someone that you do not really understand; if you try to serve someone you don't understand, you can become a benevolent oppressor." Wow! If you try to help someone that you do not know- I mean you can help by giving people change; you can help someone push their car if their car has stalled in the middle of an intersection, of course- but if you're investing in someone's life, if you are seeing them on a regular basis- if you are trying to serve them and help them without really taking the time to find out who they are, and understand their problems, then you could do more harm than good. Helping can sometimes hurt.

You can scar these people, sometimes you could push them deeper into their shells, or push them away. For example, I had so many people in my life who hurt me. They saw me as a project. They saw me as someone who needed to be fixed. People slapped all these solutions on me and sent me to all these people, but very few people ever took the time to find out what I was going through.

I really just wanted to be loved, I wanted to be embraced, I wanted to be helped, I wanted someone to believe in me. To be sure, my mother believed in me, but we had so many challenges at home. I just wanted someone to believe in me, someone to push me, someone to see my value, someone to see my worth.

It was those people who took the time to find out who I was. It was those people who took the time to meet me on my level, and it was those people who really helped me. They changed my life.

If you are going to reach anyone, you are going to have to start by building a healthy relationship with them. You're going to have to start by opening your heart, and working on you. You are going to have to start by preparing yourself to address any issues in your own life and in your own background that could be in the way of you making a difference.

You have to address the lens through which you see the world, so that you can position yourself to develop healthy relationships.

Openness, acceptance, trust, learning, understanding, competence, commonality, charisma, dynamism and serving. Those attributes are really steps we must take to develop real relationships with others.

Now I know that's a lot. I'll be the first to admit I am growing in all of these areas. It takes work- it takes hard work- to improve and grow. The hardest thing to do in the world is to change. How are you going to change anyone else if you don't first change yourself?

I think if you change yourself-if we change ourselves- we better position ourselves to become change agents.

CHAPTER 14: ENGAGEMENT

In the last chapter, I told you that the first step in trying to reach a young person is to build relationships with them. But after you have done that, by understanding them–by seeking to understand them–, by feeling the weight of their pains and their burdens; by trying to put yourself in their shoes, you will soon recognize that you cannot stop there. Relating to young people just for the sake of having a relationship with them is good, but not enough.

After you have established rapport, you need to engage them on a deeper level. What do I mean by that? You need to engage young people that you are trying to reach by asking questions. You see, before you try to reach into someone else's life to try to make a difference in his life, you need to pause and try to find out who they are and exactly what it is that might be going through. Before you try to go in like Superman, or Superwoman, you need to pause and get a lay of the land. While this might seem like common sense to you, there are many people who don't take the time to actually sit down with someone who is in trouble to learn about what is going on. In essence, those who are most effective at reaching me were able to engage me on my level, and learn about me, on my level. They did that by humbling themselves, and asking questions. They became students of me. They were genuinely curious about me and my life. If you are going to reach anyone, you need to be willing to walk into their lives and engage them in their world. You need to be able to do something that gets their attention.

When was the last time you went into a store, and the you were just walking around minding your own business, and a salesperson walked up to you and started trying to sell something to you? They started trying to push something on you. Before ever getting a sense of what you were looking for, or before ever pausing to try to figure out whether or not you were looking for some pants; whether not you were looking for some shirts; or, whether not you were trying to buy a certain pair of shoes, they tried to pressure you into buying something. Has that ever happened to you? Before ever stopping to greet you genuinely, or at least make themselves available to you, have they tried to pressure you to buy something? Remember their their posture, their tone of voice? When you walked into the story, they probably gave you that "purchased" smile that hints they are only smiling at you because they want your money, not because they are genuinely interested in helping you meet your needs.

In the same way, so many people who claim they want to help young people often walk in with a prepackaged solution to that young person's problem without ever trying to establish a relationship with that person. Because of this common mistake being made by many people who work with young people, I think it is absolutely essential for you to be able to walk into a person's life not as someone who is a guru who has all the answers. You don't want to walk in someone else's life with all of your prepackaged solutions and just lay them on them. Seriously, you need to put yourself in the position to become a listener. When in comes to trying to help youth, you don't want to be like that. Yes, I believe there comes a time to put pressure on them, but not at this phase- not yet.

Before you present any solutions, I think you would do well to engage young people with questions in order to assess their needs. You need to learn how to open the conversation. You need to learn how to approach them. You need to get their attention in a way that they don't feel threatened. What is the best way to do that? One of the best ways to engage anyone is to ask them a question. Sometimes, the best way to meet somebody you don't know is to not only greet them, but ask them a question about themselves.

I want to make a comment here about the difference between motivation and manipulation. What you're trying to do is not manipulate young people. Manipulation is when you try to get someone else to do something because it is going to benefit you; motivation, however, is when you are trying to introduce something into that person's life in order to improve their conditions. Motivation is when you have THEIR best interests at heart. You're not trying to manipulate them, you're trying to motivate them. There is a difference.

Manipulation benefits you; motivation benefits them. Are you trying to reach them so you look good, or are you trying to reach them so that their lives improve? Motivation involves you trying to make that person's life better. You are trying to improve their personal circumstances. You are trying to give that person a sense of joy, a sense of happiness, or a sense of purpose. In order to do that, you need to somehow make sure you are trying to motivate people rather than manipulate them.

What are some questions you can ask to engage people on their levels? I believe there are questions that need to be asked on several different levels, but let's start with something very basic. Sometimes just walking up to a young person that you are trying to establish a relationship with, and simply greeting them with a question like, "how's it going?" is perfectly appropriate. If you know the person, then you might even be able to get a little more personal with a question like,"is everything okay?"

I think it's important here to make a distinctions: What you must do to engage an individual is a little different from trying to engage an entire group of people. For the rest of this chapter, I'll first share my thoughts on ways to engage an individual. Then in the next chapter, I'll try to explain my views on how to engage groups. I have had a lot of experience walking into a room of strangers, and trying to engage them on their levels. Here are some of the things that you might want to consider when engaging individuals.

WAYS TO ENGAGE INDIVIDUALS

There is a difference between two types of young people that you will be dealing with: someone that you already have a relationship with, and someone that you do not know. If you're dealing with a person that you have some kind of history with, then it's more appropriate for you to be able to walk into that person's life in a more informal manner and simply greet them with, "is everything okay?" "Hey, you look like you have something on your mind. Is everything okay?" Or, "hey man, you seem like there's something going on. I see it in your eyes. If you ever want to talk, you know where to find me."

The conversation can start off as simply as that. Sometimes those questions will open up an opportunity for you to really hear what's going on in this young person's life. You see, it's easier for you to have these kinds of conversations with young people that you have had a relationship with. And that leads me to my next point: you would do well to be the kind of person who is known as a friend to young people. It would be nice if you had a reputation of being someone who cares about young people. The go-to person, if you will. You know, the person that young people can go to whenever they have problems, or whenever they need someone to talk to. It would be nice if you had a reputation of being that kind of person, the person who is so warm, who exudes a welcoming attitude- someone who greets them with love in your eyes. If you're that person, I guarantee you will have no shortage of young people in your life seeking your advice, seeking your affirmation, seeking to be in your very presence, simply because of the love that's flowing from your heart.

But let's say you are in a new situation, and you are around a new group of young people. What do you do then? Or let's say you're walking down the street and you see a young man sitting on a park bench. What in the world could you say or do to get his attention? This leads me into my discussion about the second kind of young person that you will be dealing with. There are some young people who will come into your life that you do not know, and you do not have any history with. You have no idea about their past or their present; all you know is you want to help them have a future they can call their own. There is a burden in your heart for that young person, because you can sense that there's something going on in that person's life. And, you may sense he or she may need help.

You need to ask questions about the person. Something safe and unique or interesting about them. When you engage a young person, you need to look for body language, shoes, clothes- anything that will allow you to establish an immediate connection. When you walk up to a young person, you can simply say something like "Man, those are some nice shoes you have on. What are they called?" "Man you got a nice cut, where'd you go to get your cut?" Or you can ask something more indirect like, "Hey man, can you help me? I'm trying to find the nearest (insert whatever might need be nearby)?"

You want to start by expressing something that shows that you are sincerely interested in the individual as a person. Remember you're already relating to this young person. Now you want to find a way to simply ask a question that will get his or her attention. You can start asking questions that will help you assess this person's needs. But in order to do that, sometimes you can be very direct, whereas other times you need to be more subtle. In any case, your main goal here is to assess the needs of the young person that your dealing with. You're trying to figure out what may be wrong.

You're trying to get a sense of who this young person is. You want to understand what's going on at home. You want to get an understanding of what school he or she goes to.

Questions to find out a little bit more about someone:

You want to then begin assessing really what's something that might motivate this young person. You need to think of a list of questions that will help you meet these kids right where they are. And you need to rehearse them over and over again so that they come and they feel natural. You want to come off as natural.

I recommend you start off on generally safe questions, then slowly ease into more personal questions. Also, I recommend you start with questions about the young person's identity first, then ask questions about their goals and dreams and finally their obstacles. There is no formula. You have to find things that work for you. These are things that have worked for me.

So, I think you should first ask general life questions, then dream questions, then obstacle questions. That way, the conversation progresses toward you being able to get a better sense of their perception about themselves and the world around them.

Here are some questions you can use to begin thinking of your own questions.

Questions to Start the Conversation:

- How did your family get to this area?
- What do you do for fun? Do you like riding your bike, playing video games, camping, wrestling, shopping?
- Do you have any pets? If so, what kind? What's his/her name?
- How did you get into _____? (Football, rapping, etc.)
- Do you like living in _____?
- Do you know your father? Do you have a relationship with him?
- Are you happy?
- Do you have a car?

- Do you have a job?

- Are you okay?

- You have any brothers or sisters?

- Are you on Facebook? Twitter?

- Have you ever been to a baseball game?

- Are you from this area? Is your family from this area?

Questions to Take the Conversation to a Deeper Level

- How is your relationship with your father and mother?

- What's going on at home?

- How are you doing in school?

- What grade are you in?

- What do you do when you're not in school?

- What neighborhood do you live in?

- How long have you been in this area? This school? This state?

- How long have you _____ (pick any topic that might be of interest to them).

- How long have you and him/her been talking, or going together (I.e. Been in a relationship)

- Would you tell me about your family? How many siblings do you have

- Other than doing _____, what other sports, hobbies, etc, have you tried?

Questions about Dreams and Goals:

- Do you want to be a professional athlete?

- You play sports?

- Do you want to go to college?

- You want to travel the world?

- You do want to own your own house?

- Do you want to drive a nice car?

- You want to make a lot of money?

- You want to be able to buy your mom a brand new house?

- What were you goals last year? Did you achieve them?

- In the past, did you achieve most of your goals?

- What are your plans for the future?

- What is your dream?

- What kind of house do you want to live in when you grow up?

- What is your vision for your life?

- What is your dream?

- Who do you want to be when you grow up?

- What are your personal goals for the year?

- How did you pick those as your top goals?

- Why did you pick those goals?

- What were your goals last year?

- What will it mean to you when your dream becomes your reality?

- What do you want to accomplish in the next year?

- What do you plan on doing in the next six months of your life?

- What's the most important goal for you to accomplish next year? How are you doing in terms of achieving your goals?

- Did you reach last year's goals?

- What were your New Year's resolutions?

- Have your goals been realistic in the past?

- How much money do you want to make?

- What would you do if you did not need money?

- If you could go anywhere in the world where would you go?

- How much traveling have you done in your life?

- Why do you want to travel?

- What kind of life do you want for your children?

- How are you going to pay for that kind of life?

- What school would you like to attend?

- What's your favorite college?

- Do you have any money saved up in your bank account?

- Do you have a bank account?

- How many children do you want?

- Do you want a big home?

- Of all your goals, which is your most important goal this year? Which one do you want to achieve more than the others?

- What would you do if you did not need money?

- What do you plan on doing to achieve that goal?

- How do you determine whether you are getting closer to your goals?

- When do you plan on achieving your goal? Dream? What is your deadline?

- If you could go anywhere in the world, where would you go?

- Where do you want to go to college?

- How much money does it cost per year to go to that school?

- How much money do you have saved up for college?

- What kinds of things would you like to have in your dream home?

- How much money do you want to make every month? Every year?

- What kinds of things would you buy if you were financially free?

Questions to Identify Obstacles

- What is preventing you from becoming what you want to be?

- Have you designed a plan to overcome your challenges?

- What must you have to overcome in order for your dreams to be realized?

- Why haven't you achieved your goals yet?

- What obstacle in your life is the most crucial to overcome?

- Are you making the progress necessary to overcome the obstacles that you have in your life?

- What are some things you can do to start overcoming some of these obstacles in your life?

Remember, your goal in asking these questions is to to get a sense of who this young person is. You are not trying to be a psychologist; you're trying to be a friend.

It's at this point in the conversation that you are beginning to get a sense of who the young person is, and where this young person has been, where this young person wants to go, the kind of person he or she wants to become; and, the kinds of obstacles that are keeping him or her from realizing those dreams. It's at this point that you can get a really good sense of the needs that this young person has.

While he or she is answering your questions, you need to be thinking about what this kid's greatest hopes and needs are. Does he have father issues? Has his father been gone his whole life? Does he even know who his father is? Does this kid have a bad, self-defeating attitude? If so, try to get at the root of why he has a bad attitude?

I can't stress enough that you're going to need patience in order to get a young attention. Is this kid homeless? Does she have an unstable home life? Has he moved from place to place to place, year after year, and doesn't have really any roots in any one community? Does this kid have a drug problem? Does he smoke marijuana? Busy selling drugs? Does her neighborhood have lots of gangs? Does he wear clothes that might indicate he's involved in gang activity?

Can she form a sentence properly? Is he always tired? Does this kid seem like he needs to see a counselor? Is this young person suicidal? Is she depressed? Does this person have low self-esteem? Is this young person in need of love? Is this young person sleeping around with different people in order to find some kind of love or affirmation? Does this person wear a lot of makeup because she don't think she's pretty or attractive? Does this young person have a hard time making eye contact with you?

Does the young person hang out in your classroom long after school gets out? That might be an indication that this young person doesn't want to go home, which might tell you that there are some problems at home? This would be a good opportunity for you to ask questions about that. All of these aforementioned issues give you a good sense of the kinds of things that this young person is going through.

What's important here is that you assess where this young person is by engaging them with relevant, genuine questions.

You don't want to conduct an interview, you want to have an inner-view in which you get an inner, intimate look into the life of this young person.

In my case, I dropped out of high school and was sitting on a park bench. I was thinking of what I could do to be locked up and become just like my father. Mark Stokes walked up to me, and engages me with the question: "hey man, what you doing out here on the school day?" He expected an answer, a response. But he didn't have a judgmental tone; he seemed like he was genuinely curious. He seemed like a big brother asking a younger brother a question. And, his demeanor-concerned, patient, calm- made him look like someone I could trust.

So I answered his question. He was trying to establish a common ground with me. That question was enough to get my attention. He seemed like he just wanted to have a conversation. He started sharing a little bit about himself, and he let me know that he understood my pain. He asked me questions like, "man, where's your father?" I told him my father was locked up. He asked me where my mom was; I told him that mom was at home and mom was struggling. His questions gave him a sense of who I was, and what I was going through.

From my responses to his questions, Martin could discern that I did not have a place where I felt loved. Martin could sense that I may have had father issues, because my father had been gone for all of my life. He recognized that I was not truly happy. He probably noticed I was tired. I'm pretty sure that while we were talking, he was thinking about ways to help me.

I need to say this again: you are there to come off as a friend who genuinely cares about the person. You're there to be a listening ear. You're there to show that you're the kids number one fan. You're there to be their advocate. You're on their team. You want the best for them.

You can simply pause and just spend time being very present with them, letting them know that you care about them, letting them know but you are there to listen. While you are listening, try to assess exactly what the young person needs.

CHAPTER 15: ENGAGING A GROUP

In an earlier chapter, I told you that the first step in trying to reach a young person is to build a relationship with them. But after you have related to them, by understanding them–by seeking to understand them–, by feeling the weight of their pain and their burdens, by trying to put yourself in their shoes, you will so recognize that you cannot stop there. Relating to young people, just for the sake of relating to them, is not enough. So you must engage them.

In the last chapter I talked about engaging the individual in order to find out who they are, and ultimately, what they need.

In this chapter, I'd like to share my thoughts on engaging an entire group. There are huge differences between engaging an individual and a group. Each situation has its own challenges. Maybe you are a teacher, or a small group leader, or someone who leads a group or an organization or a team, and you would like to know what you can do to reach a group.

To engage anyone, especially a group, you have to be creative. You just have to do some things that take a little courage.

MUSIC

Right off the bat, you can always use music to get the group's attention. You can watch a video, listen to a song, sing a song, rap, or play the song yourself. If you can sing or play an instrument, or rap, you can use those talents to engage your kids. They will perk up, laugh, and get with you.

If you are not comfortable with your singing voice, you can still recite the lyrics to one of your favorite songs, and unpack the meaning for the group. Or, you can have them try to explain the meaning of the song to you.

Or, you can watch MTV, or BET, or google the top 100 songs in the country to find out what kind of music kids are listening to. You can also ask them directly: who are you guys listening to? Who is your favorite rapper, singer, performer? Who is your favorite group? What is your favorite song? They will tell you what they like, and you can use that as a starting point.

TELEVISION and MOVIES

You can use scenes from shows and movies to introduce or illustrate a point you want to make. You can use those things to open your lesson plan. You can use those things to engage the young people. Find out what is popular on television, and use it as a starting point for your lesson plan. Or, you could use it to illustrate one of your points.

ENVIRONMENT

You could set up your room differently. You can arrange the chairs in a circle, or put them against the wall and have everyone sit on the floor.

Or you could put posters and pictures on the walls that are interesting or unique or poignant.

If you are outside, you could start a campfire, or something that is exciting and different.

ROLE PLAY

If you are discussing an issue have each participant tell a story that is relevant to the topic, relevant to the subject or theme or issue. Role playing involves having each participant tell a different part of the story, sharing a different perspective.

BEHAVIOR MODELING

You could also do behavior modeling, by having your students practice a skill using a four step method: You do it for them; you do it with them; they do it alone while you observe them; you give them feedback about what you observed.

CASE STUDIES

Have participants tell them about a problem, (written or verbally), then ask them to identify the issues, analyze that situation, brainstorm some possible solutions to the problem, and then propose what they recommend be done to address the problem.

You can do case studies on a drive-by shooting or about a controversial policy. In fact, you can talk about anything you want. You can present it in a way that forces them to address the problem personally. You can say something like, "If someone walked into your, living room and they had this problem (name problem), and this is their background, and these are resources you have to work with (tell them about their resources), what would you recommend for this person? What would you recommend be done in order to help that person?

These are just examples of case studies. Use them.

DEBATE

You can use debates in your classroom or with your group. Pick a Resolution like, "Students should be required to wear uniforms in school." Then form two teams (2 people on each team). One group argues in support of the Resolution. The second group argues against it. They take turns presenting their arguments, while the rest of the class takes notes and prepares questions to ask at the end of the debate.

For Resolutions, you can pick any topic. You can pick the same topics from the presidential elections; you can pick a topic you know about; you can talk about cloning; you could talk about music, you can talk about style, about language, politics, or whatever is a hot topic.

Give them time to prepare for the debate. Then, on the day of your debate, set up your classroom like it is a debate hall. Introduce the Resolution, then each team (they can have a group name), and then get the debate underway: "I'd like to call upon the first speaker of the affirmative (speaker's name) to open the debate." Someone argues the affirmative case. Someone argues the negative. Then you call for the 2nd Affirmative, then the 2nd Negative. Then the 3rd Affirmative and 3rd Negative.

Let the class observe and let these two teams go at it. You would be surprised and impressed at the things that your kids come up with, and you'll probably get no shortage of laughs from some of the things that these young people will come up with. It is a beautiful thing when you see young people sharing their ideas creatively and with passion. You may discover a future lawyer or politician or leader.

DIALOGUE

Have two people hold a conversation while the other participants observe, and ask questions. Let two people talk in front of the class about an issue and then let others discuss it and ask questions. The entire class can inform the conversation or just move the conversation along. Ask speakers for clarification, ask them to go deeper, ask them what they mean, and to defend their point(s). Ask questions that might challenge their position, or just allow the discussion to take place. Use the Socratic Method: ask questions of everyone in your class and make sure everyone participates. If someone asks a question and the person doesn't know the answer to the question, let the class chime in, or maybe you can chime in, or you can give them a little hint.

DRILLS

Use some drills where students repetitively practice a skill. Maybe it is some task that you want them to do, maybe it's passing out papers at the beginning of the class. You might want to help them learn to do that effectively, because doing that well can can save you hours of instruction time. It can give you more time to focus on lesson plans and spend less time passing out paperwork and handouts. Practice a skill. Have them go through it at the beginning of the class, or even on the first day of class.

FIELD TRIPS

Allow young people to experience the world outside of school. Expose them to more. I believe exposure is the birthplace of big dreams and motivation. Take them to a location to observe tasks being performed. The trip can be carefully planned with regard to learning objectives so that it is both fun and educational. My teacher took us on a few field trips. We once went to the Museum of Tolerance in Los Angeles, and that museum had no small impact on me and my classmates.

We went to see Schindler's List, we went to DreamWorks Studio and met Steven Spielberg. We met to UC Irvine and met Thomas Keneally, the author of Schindler's list. We went to Pomona College and the Claremont Colleges, where we were able to experience college firsthand. Those field trips were quite formative for me and my classmates.

If you are working with kids who who are despondent or disinterested, you may want to expose them to new things through field trips. You might even want to do so in smaller groups. The more difficult the child, the more attention they will need. So, taking a group of 3-5 youth to a college campus, or to an event, might go a long way in opening their hearts and mind to you.

I've met young people in almost every major city in the United States, and many of them have never left the neighborhoods in which they were born. They've never left that little enclave to see the big-city downtown. I've met young people who live on the south side of Chicago who have never been downtown, to the magnificent mile. Growing up in Long Beach, I've met people who have never been to LA. In fact, growing up, I didn't go to LA.

It took a teacher to expose me to more than rapping, rebounding, and robbing. It took a teacher to take me to a college campus in order to help me see that college was a possibility for me- that I was college material. It took a teacher to take me to nicer restaurants. She exposed us to more, and that exposure helped us want more, and inspired us to work for more; and, it positioned us to achieve more.

CHAPTER 16: AWARENESS

The "A" in R.E.A.C.H. stands for awareness. It's not enough to establish rapport with them, to build a relationship with them, though that's crucial. It's not enough to engage them on their level so that we can identify and assess their needs and their issues and their problems and their challenges-though that's vital. What's as important than those two things is to help the young people you want to reach to become AWARE of the imbalances in their lives.

Let me ask you a question: why do most people fail to lose the weight they want to lose? Or, why don't most people follow through on the goals that they set? Why don't most people keep their New Year's resolutions they make on December 31st? Why don't people follow through on commitments that they make? I think it is because of one or two reasons.

I believe everyone is motivated by two things: their desire to avoid pain and their desire to gain pleasure. I believe people are motivated by pain and pleasure.

Everything we do is motivated by the pain or the pleasure we link to it mentally. Think about it. Think of everything you have done in your life, good and bad. I bet most of your actions and decisions have been deeply rooted in either your desire to gain pleasure, or your desire to avoid pain. Why do you go to work everyday? Why do you go shopping at Christmas? Why do you wear make-up? Why are you in the relationship that you are in? Why do you hang out with that group? Pain or pleasure, that's why.

When it comes to change, young people are the same way. Therefore, we need to link pain and pleasure to the behaviors and the attitudes and the actions for our young people. They need to feel these their own imbalances for themselves. Why? Because people won't change because they feel like it. People don't change because they think it's a good idea. People change because they have to. They change because they must.

Until people get to a place where they realize they have to change, they will not change. You have to get to a place where you're sick and tired of being sick and tired.

There's was a man walking by a junk yard, and he saw a dog sitting outside of the junk yard, howling. It's obvious the dog was in pain. So the man walks into the junk yard office, and said, "there's a dog outside, and he's howling. Is he your dog?"

"Yeah, yeah…he's mine. He's sitting on a nail, " the owner replied.

Confused, the good samaritan asked, "then why doesn't he get up, off of the nail?"

To that, the owner said, "Oh he will, when it hurts bad enough."

Some of our young people are sitting on a nail. They might be complaining about the nail, and crying about the nail. But they will never get up off the nail until it hurts bad enough. Therefore, our job is simply to help them become more painfully aware of the nails in their lives.

How can you use pain and pleasure in your lesson plans? How can use pain and pleasure in your one-on-one meetings? How can you get leverage in these situations? Now I want to share three questions with you that have helped me get leverage over my own life and help me reach young people to help them get leverage over their own lives.

Three questions: what have you missed out on because of your behavior, that belief, or your attitude? What are you missing out on because of your behavior, belief, or attitude? What will you miss out on because this behavior, belief, or attitude?

Their responses are pretty telling. They have missed out on getting good grades, having healthy relationships. They are missing out on opportunities. They will not go to college, or get a good job, or be able to buy a nice house, or travel, or help people. The answers are always pretty powerful.

If you want to help anyone change, it is important for you to help them become keenly aware of the imbalances in their lives. It is important for you to help them get leverage over their situations by linking pain to the bad things and pleasure to the good things. If you want to get them to succeed, you have to help them link pain to procrastination, and link pleasure to the hard work. You have to help them link pain to missing school, and link pleasure to your classroom or location. You have to help them link pain to watching too much tv, and pleasure to reading a good book.

You have to help them link pain to talking back in class, or being disrespectful; and link pleasure to showing up early, being fully present in class, and doing homework as soon as school is out. You must link pleasure to it.

So, begin thinking how can you use pain and pleasure in your lesson plans. How can you use pain and pleasure to help them feel the imbalances in their lives?

QUESTIONS

- I think one of the best ways to help people feel the pain in their lives is by asking them questions. Here are some examples:

- What is preventing you from being where you want to be?

- What is in the way of you picking up your grades?

- What is in the way of you graduating from high school?

- What are some of the issues you have to deal with that are limiting your potential?

- Have you designed a plan to overcome the obstacles you are facing?

- What are you doing to overcome _____(specific obstacle)?

- What are you doing to overcome your bad grades?

- Which issues are you facing that have been the most difficult to overcome?

- What are some things you have tried to overcome these obstacles/challenges?

- What have you done to address these challenges? Have any of them worked?

- Questions like these will put you in position to give them the solutions they need to turn their lives around.

TELL THE TRUTH

Only after you have asked questions, and earned the right to ask hard questions, can you then point out, or at least suggest some imbalances that are there. Yes, sometimes you need to flat out share something truthful in a loving way. Make sure that what you are saying is absolutely true before you say it though, or else you could lose credibility with the young person.

Let me give you an example of how telling the truth can help one become aware of his or her imbalances. I weighted 165 pounds when I graduated from high school. In college, I played a little football for a couple years, and got up to 185 pounds of mostly muscle. When I stopped playing football, I got up to about 195 pounds. Then, when I got married, and started enjoying my wife's cooking, I got up to 200 pounds.

Then, over the last ten years, I somehow gained a lot more weight.

For years, I jogged occasionally, but not regularly. I ate whatever I wanted, and gained a little weight. But, I never thought it was a problem. I thought I still looked good, that I was still strong and healthy. After all, I played college football!

Well, a little while ago, I went to my doctor for a physical. Knowing that they were going to weigh me, I wore my lightest clothes. I was hoping that I could take off a few pounds just by the clothes I was wearing. I weighed a whopping 235 pounds! I'm not tall enough to weigh that much, but, to be honest, I really didn't think it was a problem.

The nurses also took my blood pressure, and checked my blood.

When my doctor walked into the room, we talked for little bit about life, and about our families. Then he looked at his clipboard with my information on it, and then looked up at me, and shot straight with me–he said, "you are obese!"

I laughed; he didn't.

He said again, "you are obese! You're not even an American."

Then I really laughed. He didn't. I said, "Doc I was born in Denver, Colorado."

He replied, "No! You're not even an American! Your body mass index is 33. Americans have a body mass index of 31.

So, if you get down to 31, I can then welcome you to America. And THAT'S not a compliment my friend, because Americans are obese! You're obese!"

I just stared at him.

It got even more delightful. "You have high blood pressure, high cholesterol, and you're a black male- so you have a higher risk of getting prostate cancer. You have a family, a wife, three beautiful kids. You are traveling the world helping others, and I'm concerned that things are not looking good for your future. You might not live very well, or very long. And I'm trying to be nice."

How do you think I felt when my doctor hit me with that haymaker of truth? Quite imbalanced. I became painfully aware of what was at stake. I began to think about my family, and my wife, and my kids, and my work, and my mission. I didn't have a father, and never want my kids to experience the pain of growing up without a dad. Also, I didn't think it was fair for my wife to have to raise my kids on her own, because I was sick, or dead. I thought about not being able to see my kids grow up, graduate from high school; go to college, and graduate; to get married- I thought about not being able to walk my daughter down the aisle at her wedding; I thought about missing out on life because of my poor health, and lack of self-control, and lack of discipline. I was obese, and I was very aware of it.

In that state of awareness about my obesity, my doctor asked me a question, "if you don't get ahold of yourself, what do you think is going to happen to you? You probably don't want that, do you?"

He had me right where he wanted me- painfully aware of the imbalances in my life.

I sat in that doctor's office feeling very uncomfortable about myself and my weight. I was a little embarrassed to be talked to in that way. I was obese. "Manny Man," Mr. Popular, the one who all the ladies loved in college...is obese! "What in the world has happened to me? How did I get this out of control?" I thought.

Helping someone become aware of their imbalances is probably the most important part of reaching anyone. This chapter alone is probably worth the price of the entire book, because it lays out why people do what they do, and why they change. In that doctor's office, with such hard truth, I no longer just *wanted* to get in shape, I *had* to get in shape. I no longer just felt like losing weight was a good idea; it became an inescapable must.

When you have someone in that position, painfully aware of their imbalances, you don't have much more work to do to reach them.

CHAPTER 17: CONVINCE

Once a young person, or anyone, is experiencing pain, he or she is ready to change. When people feel an imbalance in their lives- their equilibrium has been disturbed- they are inclined to change. They are open to anything that will help them restore their equilibrium. That is where "C" in R.E.A.C.H. comes in. "C" stands for convince. We have to convince young people that there is hope. We have to convince them that education is the key to their problems. We have to convince them that a good education can restore their equilibrium. We have to convince them education can help give them back their balance. We need to help them see that what we are recommending to them meets their needs.

Now you are able to make some recommendations, now you are able to serve as an advisor, now you are able to pitch some things to them that might help them alleviate their pain; to alleviate or remove or ameliorate their problem. This is where you have to convince them. We must convince them that school is a better way. We must convince them that it is important for them to do their homework.

How do you convince someone of anything? So, first, to convince someone? You lead with need. In other words, we need to lead our recommendation to them with their needs in mind. Whatever their need is, you need to think of how school, or church, or whatever, benefits THEM. You need to talk about how your recommended solution helps THEM. It is all about them. What's in it for them? What will they get out of it? How will it empower them? How will it equip them? How will it make them feel? How will it help their bank balance?

You have to sell your solution to them. You have to sell pleasure to them. You have to sell enjoyment to them. Whether you like it or not, you are in the sales business- we all are. We have to sell ideas every day, in our homes, to our spouses, to our relatives, to our kids. And to really convince anyone of anything, we need not talk about why WE like something. Instead, we have to talk about why or how it benefits THEM.

So let me ask you, what is it that you do for a living? What are you selling? What are the benefits of what you sell? Why would someone buy it from you? Write down exactly what it is you are trying to sell to the young people you want to reach.

You are not selling school; you are selling opportunity. You are not selling homework; you are selling success. You are not selling an essay; you are selling the power to communicate clearly. You are not reading; you are selling critical thinking skills, which lead to success. You get the idea. Think about what you are selling, and the benefits of it.

For example, if someone wants to play sports, you can say, "hey, if you do your homework you'll be able to pick up your grades; if you pick up your grades you'll be eligible to play sports. If you are eligible to play sports; you might be able to get a scholarship; and if you get a scholarship to go to college, you might be able to get drafted to play professional sports; even if you don't get to that level, you can still graduate from college and get a nice job, start a business, make a living and a difference." That is all about benefits.

I've found that you don't need to talk about the cost of what you're talking about, because if you give someone a big enough "Why?" they are not as concerned about the "how much?" Their desire to experience the pleasure of the benefits will motivate them to do whatever is necessary to attain those benefits.

When you are trying to convince them, you may also need to point out the pain in their lives. People do more out of fear for loss, than they will to gain some pleasure, from my experience. People work harder if they are afraid they are going to lose their jobs, than they do for a promotion.

In any case, you need to share with them your solution, share with them your recommendations. Tell them, "you need to come to this group, you need to come to class, you need to show up early," or something like that. No matter what you say, talk about the benefits of what you are asking them to do.

If a student is always running late, talk about the benefits of showing up early, and on time. Talk about the benefits of getting enough sleep at night. Talk about the benefits of getting up early to prepare their hearts and minds and their bodies for a day of productive work. Talk about the benefits of showing up to class on time. Talk about the benefits of showing up to class. Talk about the benefits of paying attention when they are in class. Talk about the benefits of being fully attentive to what their teachers and what others are saying. Talk about the benefits of doing homework before they hangout with friends, or before they start talking to the girls or guys. Talk about the benefits of reading books, of reading magazines, of writing.

If you teach math, talk about the benefits of learning equations. Whatever it is, talk about the benefits of learning whatever it is that you want them to learn. Talk about the benefits of asking for help, talk about the benefits of being able to just admit that you need help. Talk about the benefits of exercising. Talk about the benefits. I'm repeating a lot, because repetition is the mother of learning. I want you to get this. If you get this, you'll reach more youth, save more lives, make a big difference, make more money, and create a lasting legacy. You see, those are the real benefits of you reading this book. It's not about me; it's about you, and what you can get as a result of this. Your kids are the same way.

CHAPTER 18: HAND

Finally, after you have talked about the rewards, the benefits of what you are recommending, there is one important final step to reaching someone. After helping someone become aware of their imbalances, this last step may be the next most important part of this book. You see, it is not enough to present the solution to someone; It is not enough to just simply recommend that they do something. You have to ask them to accept your proposal or recommendation. You have to do your best to make a decision, a commitment.

If the man who reached me on that park bench had only told me what I needed to do, without asking me to make a decision to do it; if my teacher in high school only told me that I needed to go to college without actually asking me to make a decision - a mental purchase- to go to college, then I am almost certain that I would not have gone to college when I did, if ever. No, they asked me to make a decision- to decide- to apply their solution to my own life. They placed the ball in my court. They put the responsibility on me to change my own life. They both realized that they couldn't change me. All they could do was convince me to change myself, and they realized that my only hope for making those changes was by making a decision- by taking ownership of my life and my decisions.

Indeed, they took the last step involved in reaching me: They extended their HAND. The "H" in R.E.A.C.H. stands for hand. To reach someone, you have to extend your hand figuratively, and sometimes literally, to ask for them to make a commitment. You must ask them to make a decision.

Now I want to share with you some effective ways, some proven ways, to ask someone to make a commitment.

THE STAIR-STEP

First there is the Stair-Step. Some people have called it the ascending close. Others have called it the part-by-part close. I personally do not care what you call it. I care that you use it. The Stair-Step approach to extending your hand involves you organizing, and asking, a set of questions in ascending order that will cause the youth with whom you are speaking to say "yes." For it to be effective, you need to organize your questions carefully and organize them in ascending order so that you can ultimately lead them to make a commitment. So here is just an example of it:

"Do you want more out of life?" They better say yes.

"Do you want to be happy." Yes!

"Do you want to be fulfilled?" Yes!

"Do you want to be able to help a lot of people in your life?"

"Do you want to be successful? Yes!

"Do you want to make the most of your life?"

"Do you want better grades?" Yes

"Do you want a happy family?" Yes

"Do you want to be great?"

"Do you want to make a difference in the world?"

"Do you…" Yes! Yes! Yes!

You get the point.

Now you just keep asking these kinds of questions in ascending order. Then, when you feel that the person really means it, then you transition to the extension of your hand: "If I could show you how to do those things, would you be interested?" Yes!

"How soon would you want to get started?" RIGHT NOW!

Again, the idea is for you to ask several questions in ascending order- questions that you believe they will answer in the affirmative. Then you ask them, "how soon would you like to get started?"

Write your questions down on paper, organize them in ascending order, placing the easiest "yeses" first. Then practice asking them. Rephrase them, play with them for a little while, until you feel comfortable with them; and then ask the young person to make a commitment.

THE SANDWICH

Picture a sandwich. You have a piece of bread, you have something in the middle, and then you have another piece of bread.

When you are using The Sandwich, you're simply "sandwiching" the decision with benefits, benefit-decison-benefit. Okay, you have the decision in the middle of the two benefits. So let's say you have just laid out, you've just recommended that this kid take school seriously, that this kid picks up their grades. You've laid out an action plan.

To do so, you first start talking about the benefits with the young person. "You'll be able to pick up your grades; you'll be able to play on the team; you will be able to go on this field trip; you will be able to get X; now you'll be able to go to college…and yes you're going to have to work hard, but just think about the opportunities that are going to come; think about the money you might be able to make; think about the jobs that might be offered to you; think about the business that you want to grow; think about the people you will be able to help; think about the best places you will be able to travel…"

Then you EXTEND YOUR HAND: "Why don't you give it a try?" You sandwiched the cost between the benefits, so that they focus on the rewards of what they will be getting as opposed to what they will be losing, or what it is going to cost them in terms of work.

THE SCALE

You simply ask, "on a scale of 1 to 10- ten being you are ready to make a commitment; one being you are nowhere near ready- on a scale of 1 to 10, where are you in terms of being ready to make this decision?"

If they say anything other than 10, you simply say, "okay, you are at (# between 1-10) now; what would it take to get you to a 10?" Then, you just listen. Let them respond. Listen respectfully, and if their objections can be overcome, then respond appropriately. If you have responses to their objections, you can then EXTEND YOUR HAND: "Obviously that concern you have is not as big as you think it is. So there is really nothing in the way of you making this commitment today. So why don't you give it a try? How soon can you get started?

THE BEN FRANKLIN

You start by simply asking, "you want to make the best decision possible , right?" They usually will say yes. Then you continue, "well, why don't we try something that Benjamin Franklin used to do when he needed to make a major decision?"

Then you explain, " Benjamin Franklin he was an inventor, he was a millionaire, he was a Founding Father; and, whenever he needed to make an important decision, he used to pull out a piece of paper, draw a line down the middle, creating two columns. In the top left column, he wrote down reasons he should take a course of action; and on the top right column of that piece of paper, he wrote down reasons against making that course of action."

Then you ask your young person, "Why do not we give that a try?" Then you pull out your piece of paper, draw a line down the middle, and on the top left column, you write down "Reasons For." Then you ask the young person, "what are some reasons for you picking up your grades?" (or whatever). Then you help them make that list as long as possible. You want to help them write down the benefits of taking a certain course of action.

Then ask them, "Have we covered everything?" Once they say yes, then you slide the piece of paper over to them and say, "Now you come up with reasons against making this decision, or taking this course of action." More often than not, they will only be able to come up with two or three. In any case, YOU MUST NOT HELP THEM COME UP WITH REASONS AGAINST!

Let them come up with their reasons against making this decision. If the "Reasons For" list is really long and the Reasons Against" list is really short, you can then EXTEND YOUR HAND: "well, it looks like you have made your decision. So how soon do we want to get started?"

THE SECONDARY

This technique simply involves focusing on a minor part of your presentation. People use this on us all the time. If you are at a shoe store, and someone asks you, "would you like the size 8 or size 9?" If you respond to that question, they are assuming that you've made the purchase, and chances are that you have. You have made the purchase emotionally. When people use this approach, they are focusing on the secondary part of their presentation, never asking you if you are going to make the purchase; but which purchase you are going to make.

You can use this with young people- EXTEND YOUR HAND: "Are you going to do your math first, or work on your essay?" You've started with the end, asking them which homework assignment they're going to work on.

THE 3 QUESTIONS

Sometimes you can simply ask them three questions: 1. Can you see where this could help you pick up your grades? 2. Are you really interested in picking up your grades? 3. If you were ever going to start picking up your grades, when do you think would be the best time to start?"

THE NO

This is a short simple one you can use. All you need to do is ask, "are there any questions that you have for me?" If they say "no, you pretty much covered everything," you have to assume that they have just made a purchase. So you just go ahead and act like they just said yes. You have to act like they

just made a decision, it's the negative answer close. You
EXTEND YOUR HAND: "why don't you give it a try?

THE PROMISE ME

A little while ago, I was being recruited by two
different organizations. Both of them wanted me to come and
work for them. One organization reached out to me, and they
said, "man, we would really like you on our staff, we think
you could make a tremendous difference here. You would
have a great impact here. We just want you to come." Well,
another organization was recruiting me at about the same time.
And when I mentioned the first opportunity, they pulled me
aside and said, "Before you make a decision to go with anyone
else, would you please come and talk to me first?" They asked
me to promise them.

How can you use that with your young people?
EXTEND YOUR HAND: "Hey listen, I know you are
thinking about doing X, or I know you have the opportunity to
do X, but do this for me: before you make a decision, would
you come back to me, and talk to me before you follow
through with that decision? Would you do that for me,
please?"

THE WALK-AWAY

After you have made your strongest appeal to the
person, but the young person is not being persuaded. So, in
defeat, you shake their hand, and you say, "Thank you for

your time, you know. I appreciate you. Thank you for hearing me out. I'll see you later." Then you walk away. And as you are walking away, you turn around, and you say, "you know what? just before I go, can I ask you a question? I've done my best today, and I really, I really want to make a difference, and I feel like I just missed something; and, I don't want that to happen again in the future when I'm talking to someone else. Would you mind telling me why- what is the real reason you did not make the decision to accept what I recommended to you? Just shoot straight with me."

Then, if they oblige, and share something with you that you have an actual response to, go sit back down and you try one last time to convince them to make a decision.

There are many more ways to EXTEND YOUR HAND; I've just given you a sample here. In this chapter, I just wanted to give you several ways you can ask someone to make a decision. But the key is, you have to ask them to make a decision, you have to extend your hand- to convince them to make a commitment.

In every case, you have to appeal to their heart, you have to appeal to their minds, you have to lead with their needs by talking about the benefits, and then you need to ask them to make a decision.

Some might say this is manipulation, I do not. I believe it is persuasion. It is motivation. It is you trying to do something that is in the best interest of someone else. You get nothing more than a sense of gratitude for having helped them, but that is it. The real benefit is theirs. If that is not the case in your appeal, then you might be teetering on the edge of manipulation.

You have to have their best interest at heart. You have to be persuasive. You are selling ideas, you are selling hope, you are selling change, so you have to do everything in your power to get young people to make mental purchases.

You get young people to make mental purchases by EXTENDING YOUR HAND!

If you'll do that, if you'll extend your hand, you can change someone's entire life. If you'll extend your hand, you can reach out to someone and help them see their own infinite possibilities, and leave their souls in joyous awe; if you'll extend your hand, you can change a family, you can change an entire generation; if you extend your hand, you can change the world.

So don't let crucial moments pass without you asking them to make a decision. If you can see that they have become aware of an imbalance in their lives, then EXTEND YOUR HAND!

They might not make a purchase, mentally or emotionally on the spot, but they'll never forget you. They will probably remember the feeling they had as a result of speaking with you, and remember your hand. They'll remember your challenge. They'll remember you!

You start with building meaningful relationships. Second, you engage them with activities and questions in order to assess who they are, what they want out of life, and what is in the way of their goals and dreams. Third, you must help them become aware of the imbalances in their lives. Fourth, you begin to convince them that you have what they need. Fifth, you must extend your hand.

Just before I finish, I need to share one last thing with you. A little while ago, I was speaking at a school in the Chicago area, and after my presentation was over, my host was rushing me to the exit doors so I could head to my next presentation at another school. But on my way out of the door, a custodian stopped me, "Mr. Scott! Please, we need your help." He then led me to a bathroom. The closer I got to the bathroom door, I could hear someone crying. I looked at the custodian, and asked him, "What's wrong?" "We don't know," he said, "but he won't talk to anyone." I walked into the bathroom, and saw a tall young man bent over, sobbing. I eased over to him, and quietly asked, "Hey, buddy. My name is Manny Scott. What's wrong?"

He looked toward me, stood up, with tears pouring down his face. "Mr. Scott," he said, wiping his tears, "I was going home today to kill myself." I didn't say a word. I waited for him to keep talking.

"Two weeks ago, I walked into my living room, and I found my father hanging. My mother abandoned us a long time ago, and I don't know where she is...So I have no one. I have no one. The only person I had is now gone. I can't pay rent, I don't know where I'm going to go. I don't - I was going home today to kill myself."

I just stared, as he continued. "But as I was sneaking past the auditorium, to go home, I heard you speaking, and singing- something told me to stop, and listen. I felt compelled to listen. So for the whole presentation, I was in the back of the room, listening...Mr. Scott, I didn't know there was anyone in the world who understood my pain. I didn't believe I could make it through this pain. I'm in here crying, because you have given me a reason to keep living. You have helped me see that I can make it. That I need to keep living. That I am here for a reason. You helped me see that I can make it through the pain....Mr. Scott," he looked me directly in my eyes, "thank you! Thank you for saving my life!"

I recently received a letter from that young man. He is graduated from college, and is now doing very well.

I share that with you not to impress you, but to impress upon you that kids everywhere are hurting, and they need hope and help.

I have tried my best to share with you my best understanding of reaching youth who seem unreachable. I have given you ways to look more carefully at your own frame of reference, and at the frame of reference of your students. I have talked about what it takes to develop healthy relationships with you. We have talked about the importance of engaging them on their levels, and about helping them become painfully aware of the imbalances in their lives. We have talked about convincing them there is hope; and, now, we have talked about ways to get them to make commitments that can improve the quality of their lives. We have talked about extending your hand to help them make commitments. That's all I have so far. Now it's my time for me to do what I have asked you to do.

I now extend my hand to you...Will you commit? Now that you have made it to the end of this book, what are you going to do? Will you close this book, and return to doing things they way you have always done them? Will you go back to business-as-usual? Or, will you commit to doing something different, or trying something new? It is my hope that you renew your commitment to serve. It is my hope that you renew your commitment to speak, to teach, to coach, to lead, to serve, to love with all your heart, soul, mind, and strength. Someone else's life, and destiny is tied to your response. Please take my hand. Take this challenge, this commission, and go!

About the Author

An original Freedom Writer whose story is told in part in the 2007 hit movie, *Freedom Writers*, Manny Scott is the speaker of choice for conferences, conventions, schools, fundraisers, and banquets.

He is the founder of Ink International Incorporated, an educational consulting firm that has empowered over 1.5 million people to improve the quality of not only their own lives, but also the lives of those around them. Ink has helped hundreds of organizations raise student achievement and leader effectiveness in 47 states and four continents. Ink has helped prevent thousands of dropouts and suicides.

He is also the author of *Your Next Chapter*, a book that shows people, step-by-step, how to create the life of their dreams; and, *Turning the Page*, his not-yet-released memoir that he only makes available to people who hear him in person.

He is now happily married, a father of three, a homeschool teacher, a successful entrepreneur, a Ph.D. student, an author, an aviator, and one of the nation's most sought after speakers.

For more info and resources, contact us at:

Ink International
P.O. Box 464868
Lawrenceville, GA 30042
Phone: (888) 987-TURN
Or visit our website at:
www.MannyScott.com

32639097R00119

Made in the USA
Middletown, DE
11 June 2016